Bloom's Modern Critical Interpretations

Modern Critical Interpretations

Ray Bradbury's
Fahrenheit 451

Edited and with an introduction by
Harold Bloom
Sterling Professor of the Humanities
Yale University

CHELSEA HOUSE
PUBLISHERS
An imprint of Infobase Publishing

Bloom's Modern Critical Interpretations: Fahrenheit 451

Copyright © 2001, 2003 by Infobase Publishing
Introduction © 2001 by Harold Bloom

Chelsea House
An imprint of Infobase Publishing
132 West 31st Street
New York NY 10001

ISBN-10: 0-7910-5929-4
ISBN-13: 978-0-7910-5929-6

For Library of Congress Cataloging-in-Publication Data,
please contact the publisher.
ISBN 0-7910-5929-4

Chelsea House books are available at special discounts when
purchased in bulk quantities for businesses, associations, institutions,
or sales promotions. Please call our Special Sales Department in New
York at (212) 967-8800 or (800) 322-8755.

You can find Chelsea House on the World Wide Web at
http://www.chelseahouse.com

Contributing Editor: Tenley Williams

Printed in the United States of America

IBT 10 9 8 7 6

This book is printed on acid-free paper.

Contents

Editor's Note

My Introduction broods upon *Fahrenheit 451* as a "period piece" that goes on inhabiting diverse periods, despite its literary inadequacies.

Wayne L. Johnson celebrates Bradbury's cautionary tale as a parable of "spiritual development," while Donald Watt assimilates *Fahrenheit 451* to the genre of dystopia.

In William F. Touponce's account, both *Fahrenheit 451* and *The Martian Chronicles* are reveries adumbrating the perpetual literary theme of the double.

Susan Spencer, in this volume's best essay, compares *Fahrenheit 451* to Walter M. Miller's *A Canticle for Leibowitz*, another fantasy of textual survival. Other postwar American dystopias are invoked by David Seed, after which Kevin Hoskinson locates Bradbury's work in its Cold War context.

This volume concludes with three studies of symbolic imagery in *Fahrenheit 451*, all of them by Rafeeq O. McGiveron.

Introduction

While *Fahrenheit 451* manifestly is a "period piece," this short, thin, rather tendentious novel has an ironic ability to inhabit somewhat diverse periods. In its origins, the book belongs to the Cold War of the 1950s, yet it prophesied aspects of the 1960s, and has not lost its relevance as I consider it in the year 2000. One does not expect the full madness of a new Theological Age to overwhelm the United States, despite hearing both George W. Bush and Albert Gore proclaim (as I write this in February 2000) that they never make a decision without consulting Christ. And yet, in time, there may be no books to burn. In the Age of Information, how many will read Shakespeare or Dante?

I resort to a merely personal anecdote. A little while back, the New British Library wished to celebrate its grand instauration, and invited me to show up to help close a self-congratulatory week. At a Friday afternoon symposium, I was to make a third, in conjunction with the leading British authorities on software and on "information retrieval." After I protested that I did not know what the latter was, and knew nothing of software (having not yet learned to type), I was told that my function would be to "represent books." I declined the compliment and the invitation, while reflecting gloomily that a once-great library was betraying itself.

Rereading *Fahrenheit 451* after many years, I forgive the novel its stereotypes and its simplifications because of its prophetic hope that memory (and memorization!) is the answer. When I teach Shakespeare or American Poetry I urge my students to read and reread *Macbeth* and *Song of Myself* over and over again, until these essential works are committed to memory. Myself, I have *eaten the books* (to employ a Talmudic trope), and I repeat poems and plays to myself for part of each day. Bradbury, a half-century ago, had the foresight to see that the age of the Screen (movie, TV, computer) could destroy reading. If you cannot read Shakespeare and his peers, then you will forfeit memory, and if you cannot remember, then you will not be able to think.

1

Bradbury, though his work is of the surface, will survive as a moral fabulist. "The house will crumble and the books will burn," Wallace Stevens mournfully prophesied, but a saving remnant will constitute a new party of Memory. In our America-to-come, the party of Memory will become the party of Hope, a reversal of Emersonian terms but hardly of Emersonian values. Is there a higher enterprise now than stimulating coming generations to commit to memory the best that has been written?

WAYNE L. JOHNSON

Machineries of Joy and Sorrow: Rockets, Time Machines, Robots, Man vs. Machine, Orwellian Tales, Fahrenheit 451

Science fiction evolved from the industrial revolution that spawned notions of rockets, robots, time machines, computers, satellites, matter-transporters, and the like. Bradbury's focus nearly always remains upon the human element in his stories, but hardware is a basic element in science fiction and machines inevitably play an important role in his tales about the future.

ROCKETS

If space travel has mythic significance for Bradbury, then rockets represent the tools, the vehicles for the fulfillment of that myth. They are also wonder-inspiring objects themselves. The root of Bradbury's fascination with rockets lies not in the future, but in the past, with remembrances of Fourth of July fireworks:

> Fire exploded over summer night lawns. You saw sparkling face of uncles and aunts. Skyrockets fell up in the brown shining eyes of cousins on the porch, and the cold charred sticks thumped down in dry meadows far away.

From *Ray Bradbury*. © 1980 by Frederick Ungar.

3

We never learn much about the mechanics of Bradbury's rockets, for him they seem to be simply crystallized imagination. In "R is for Rocket," fifteen-year-old Chris sees a rocket for what it is, the fulfillment of ages of imagination and myth:

> It was a hundred years of dreaming all sorted out and chosen and put together to make the hardest, prettiest, swiftest dream of all. Every line was fire solidified and made perfect, it was flame frozen, and ice waiting to thaw there in the middle of a concrete prairie, ready to wake with a roar, jump high and knock its silly fine great head against the Milky Way.

When Bradbury does give any details about the interior workings of his rocketships, they tend to reinforce the image of a solidified dream. When Fiorello Bodoni steps into the rocket mock-up he notes: "The rocket smelled of time and distance. It was like walking into a clock. It was finished with Swiss delicacy. One might wear it on one's watch fob."

The space ship *Copa de Oro* is specially designed to sweep close enough to the sun to scoop up a piece of it. Outside the ship the sun was so hot it "burned all time and eternity away." Jules Verne might tell us in concrete detail how a ship could perform such a feat, but Bradbury does not. Instead, he portrays the ship as defying the ultimate in summery heat with a mechanically-produced season of its own:

> Through corridors of ice and milk-frost, ammoniated winter and storming snowflakes blew. Any spark from that vast hearth burning out there beyond the callous hull of this ship, any small firebreath that might seep through would find winter, slumbering here like all the coldest hours of February.

Besides ignoring the mechanics of rocketry, Bradbury pays no attention to the problems surrounding real rockets. The questions of space appropriations, air pollution, or the perversion of the technology into weapons systems are rarely, if ever, raised. To write a story about man's future among the stars requires some means of getting man to the stars in the first place. Rockets not only make possible the wonders of space travel and man's immortality, they also function as symbols for these wonders and as talismans of good fortune. Bradbury would have us stand with the couple in "The End of the Beginning" as they waited in the darkness and saw ". . . the brightening color in the sky and, ten seconds later, the great uprising comet burn the air, put out the stars and rush away in fire flight . . ." Or with Chris in "R is for Rocket" when ". . .

the Dream woke up and gave a yell and jumped into the sky." Like planes and sailing ships before them, Bradbury's rockets are objects of myth and romance. The details of how they operated or where the money came from are ultimately less important than who they carried and where they went.

TIME MACHINES

Modern science has tended to reject the possibility of time travel and so there are few theories about what a time machine would look like and how it would function. Even the classic device in H. G. Wells' *The Time Machine* is only vaguely described. Bradbury's stories about time travel tend to stress the psychological implications or the paradoxes involved, and so place little stress on machinery. Many writers have avoided the use of a machine at all, and have suggested some sort of "warp" or "fold" in the fabric of time to explain travel through this dimension. Though Bradbury does not say so explicitly in the story, some such warp seems to have taken place in "The Dragon." Actually, it is suggested that the moor on which the two knights wait is somehow immune to time. One of the knights says: "On this moor is no Time, is only Forever. I feel if I ran back on the road the town would be gone, the people yet unborn . . ."

Most of Bradbury's stories about time travel do involve a machine of some sort, though it is mentioned only in passing. Time Safari, Inc. operates a commercial time machine in "A Sound of Thunder." Eckels gets an impression of the machine just before he steps into it which is just that—impressionistic.

> Eckels glanced across the vast office at a mass and tangle, a snaking and humming of wires and steel boxes, at an aurora that flickered now orange, now silver, now blue. There was a sound like a gigantic bonfire burning all of Time, all the years and all the parchment calendars, all the hours piled high and set aflame.

This machine has a sort of accessory, a metallic antigravity path which travellers into the past walk on. The path floats above the ground and prevents the time travellers from accidentally touching any part of the world it has not been cleared to touch. As Eckels finds out, such an inadvertent contact might alter the course of evolution. These mechanical items are necessary in "A Sound of Thunder" first, to supply the means of transportation one assumes would be necessary for a safari, and secondly, to explain which paradoxes of time travel will be relevant to the story and which will not. The path, for instance, serves to isolate the incident wherein Eckels alters the future, and allows us to trace just how his misstep had its effect.

No such requirements are necessary in "Forever and the Earth," so we never glimpse the machine which transports Tom Wolfe from his deathbed into the future. Henry Field, who is responsible for the whole plan, simply says to the professor who is perfecting a time machine: "Here's a check, a blank check, fill it in." Even Wolfe has only the vaguest impressions of his trip: "I smelled electricity, I flew up and over, and I saw a brass city. I thought, I've arrived. This is the city of heaven . . ."

Another man who wishes to meddle with the fate of a dead writer builds "The Kilimanjaro Device." This is apparently a modified Land Rover: "I've seen those before . . . a truck like that in a movie. Don't they hunt rhino from a truck like that?" Since the story is essentially a fantasy, no further details are really needed, and none are given.

When Roger and Ann Kristen wish to escape the horrors of 2155 A.D., they take advantage of another professional service, Travel in Time, Inc., to flee into 1938. A government search party pursues them, armed with a time machine disguised as a motion picture camera. Here again the time machine is required merely as a prop, so little attention is given to it. Stories such as these mentioned so far are science fiction at its most abstract. They seem closest to Bradbury's concept of the "idea" story, since they derive much of their interest from the novelty of their premise. These are the most improbable of the "What if . . . ?" stories. "What if we could go back in time?" is a little like asking "What if two plus two equalled five?" The trappings of science could add a touch of verisimilitude to what, after all, could only be accomplished by magic. A fine heavy machine serves as a kind of anchor, stabilizing some rather flighty speculation, and freeing us to enjoy the puzzles and paradoxes of an impossible situation. But there is another kind of time travel, one that is real enough. This is the journey through memory, a journey we may all take through our own past, and one we may share with others. For Bradbury, this is a special kind of time travel, combining as it does reality and imagination in an intriguingly ambiguous way. If time travel is viewed as a function of memory, then a human being can be a time machine. This is indeed the case with Colonel Freeleigh in *Dandelion Wine*. Objects that arouse or reinforce the function of memory can also be time machines. In this respect, the attic in "A Scent of Sarsaparilla" is Bradbury's most elaborate and finely drawn time machine:

> Consider an attic. Its very atmosphere is Time. It deals in other years, the cocoons and chrysalises of another age. All the bureau drawers are little coffins where a thousand yesterdays lie in state. Oh, the attic's a dark, friendly place, full of Time.

This attic, which Mr. Finch visits on cold November afternoons, is a massive and elaborate machine. Its controls are many and complex. Yet, because it works directly through the senses, Bradbury is able to portray exactly how it functions. It is a thing of sound: "The attic . . . creaked every bone and shook down ancient dusts." And silence: "The attic was quiet as a thundercloud before a storm." Of light: "His flashlight caught and flickered [chandelier prisms] alive, the rainbows leapt up to curve the shadows back with colors, with colors like plums and strawberries and Concord grapes, with colors like cut lemons and the sky where the clouds drew off after storming." And scent: "The dust of the attic was incense burning and all of time burning."

Finch knows how to operate this machine because he, after all, is the one who built it. The motivation is there in Finch's desire to escape the winter of age and return to the summer of youth. The seasons are obvious symbols in the story, but the central symbol is a sensual experience, the scent of sarsaparilla wafting in through the attic window to call Finch back to the days of his youth. Finch need only put his time machine into operation to return to that long-ago summer:

> If you touched prisms here, doorknobs there, plucked tassels, chimed crystals, swirled dust, punched trunk hasps and gusted the vox humana of the old hearth bellows until it puffed the soot of a thousand ancient fires into your eyes, if, indeed, you played this instrument, this warm machine of parts, if you fondled all of its bits and pieces, it levers and changers and movers, then, then, *then*!

This attic time machine is not so different from Bradbury's rockets. Both types of machine are crystallizations of human imagination, dreams drawn out of the mind and made solid. Each machine is also a metaphor for the stories in which they are found, stories born in Bradbury's mind and realized on the page. The stories, like the machines, take us on a journey through time, space, or a change of season. As in the tales involving magic, Bradbury's consciousness of his own craft is very close to the surface of these stories.

ROBOTS

Few concepts have captivated the imaginations of science fiction writers and their audience as the robot has. The significance of the robot goes far beyond that of a mere mechanical contrivance. In the world of science fiction, the robot represents the ultimate heart of the scientific conceit, wherein man's knowledge of the universe becomes so great that he is able to play God and create other men. So powerful is this idea, and so laden is it with mythical implications, that science fiction has rarely been able to treat the robot realistically. The term robot comes from the Czech *robota* meaning compulsory labor. The name as applied to mechanical men was first popularized in 1921 through Czech playwright Karl Capek's expressionistic drama *R. U. R. (Rossum's Universal Robots)*. *R. U. R.* contains many classic elements of the robot story as explored by later writers, including Bradbury. In particular, Rossum's robots look exactly like human beings and can be wired to think rationally, even to feel emotions. This leads to the inevitable problems which arise when man creates man. At one point in the play, Helena Glory is so impressed by the robots' resemblance to human beings, that she cannot quite decide how to refer to them, until the manager of the robot factory corrects her:

> HELENA. I saw the first robots at home. The town council bought
>   them—I mean engaged them for work.
> DOMAIN. Bought them, dear Miss Glory. Robots are bought
>   and sold.

Bradbury has created his own robot factory, Marionettes, Inc., whose customers, like those of Rossum's, tend to come to unhappy ends. Bradbury's robots, like Rossum's, look like human beings. Bradbury's characters often come to grief through allowing the difference between a man and a robot to become blurred. Several stories are less than successful due to a similar fuzziness of distinction on Bradbury's part between man and machine.

"Marionettes, Inc." is a horror story as well as a light-hearted warning against taking robots for granted. Braling achieves the dream of the dominated married man and substitutes a mechanical replica of himself to keep his wife occupied while he enjoys a night out with Smith. Braling confides in Smith that he is planning a vacation in Rio, during which the robot will fill in at home with his unsuspecting wife. Smith is awed by the details of Braling's plan as he peruses some of Marionettes, Inc.'s literature. As the literature points out, " . . . while an act is pending in Congress to legalize Marionettes, Inc., it is still a felony, if caught, to use one." This punitive attitude toward the robots seems directed at their potential for facilitating illicit pleasure rather than at their possible use in fraud. Even the company's motto: "No Strings Attached," seems to bear this out. In any case, Braling comes to a suitable comeuppance at the hands of his mechanical double, while Smith, having succumbed to Braling's temptations, receives an unpleasant shock of his own. (Men named Braling have unfortunate experiences with machines in Bradbury's stories. In "Wake for the Living"—not in any of the major Bradbury collections—one Richard Braling comes to grief while investigating his brother's mechanical coffin.)

The use of human-like robots for mere gratification, whether sexual or otherwise, continues to be frowned upon in "Punishment without Crime." In this story, George Hill attempts to relieve his rage toward his cheating wife by murdering her robot duplicate. Marionettes, Inc. duplicates Hill's wife and her bedroom to perfection. So perfect is the robot that Hill is at first reminded only of the love he and his wife once shared. Hill tries to talk of other matters, but the robot has been programmed with a specific purpose in mind, and so works to arouse his jealous rage. Hill has, after all, paid for this experience. The parallels between the setting at Marionettes, Inc. and a brothel are not lost on Hill, and he briefly demurs:

> "Come to business, then," she said, coldly. "You want to talk to me about Leonard."
> "Give me time, I'll get to it."
> "Now," she insisted.
> He knew no anger. It had washed out of him at her appearance. He felt childishly dirty.

Hill finally does kill the robot, then is subsequently arrested and tried for murder under the "live robot" law. Hill is condemned to death and, at least at first, he accepts the verdict. He knows that objectively he has done nothing wrong, yet he is overwhelmed with guilt:

> After all, they can't let murder be legal. Even if it's done with machines and telepathy and wax. They'd be hypocrites to let me get away with my crime. For it *was* a crime. I've felt guilty about it ever since. I've felt the need of punishment. Isn't that odd?

These are lightweight stories, still they touch upon issues which Bradbury is constantly bringing up in his work. The robots are not people, yet if they are regarded as real, either mistakenly or deliberately, they can produce reactions that are perfectly genuine. Robots are products of invention, they are walking dreams. Like rockets, time machines and short stories, they are made by human hands. But their relationship to us is ambiguous, they generate as many fantasies as they fulfill. Their ultimate value may depend upon our attitude towards them, and the extent to which they stimulate our imaginations.

Three of Bradbury's robot stories are less than successful. They involve robots created as acts of homage to specific people (George Bernard Shaw, Abraham Lincoln, a family's grandmother). Unfortunately, all three stories confuse the homage due to the original person with that given to the robot. Also, the main characters of all three stories make the same mistakes in their attitudes toward robots as Hill did. They accept robots as genuine surrogates for human beings, and in so doing, have their emotional development arrested or thwarted.

In "G. B. S.—Mark V," Charles Willis spends all of his free time aboard a space ship conversing with a robot replica of George Bernard Shaw. Willis is one of Bradbury's loners, passionately committed to his own fantasy world, mocked and misunderstood by his fellow crewmen. But unlike other Bradbury heroes, Willis does not find an outlet for his fantasies in creative behavior. Instead, Willis becomes increasingly attached to what is, after all, a preprogrammed machine. At one point in the story, Willis exclaims, "Oh . . . How I wish I had been alive when you were alive, sir. How I wish I had *truly* known you." The robot answers, "*This* Shaw is best. . . . All of the mincemeat and none of the tin. The coattails are better than the man. Hang to them and survive." An unintentionally ironic assertion, since Willis is plainly talking to the tin and not the mincemeat. Of course the robot means that he represents the quintessence of Shaw's intelligence and wit, with none of the actual man's mortality. But it is in this disregard for the mortality of the original person that this, and the two stories discussed next, stray from the humanistic viewpoint characteristic of most of Bradbury's work. All of the robots aboard the space ship have been placed there for the diversion of the crewmen during the long voyage. The rest of the crew entertains itself with robot women, ". . . all the happy male bees in their hives with their syrupy wind-up soft-singing nimble-nibbling toys, their bright female puppets." Bradbury implies that Willis' conversing with the Shaw robot is a more worthwhile activity, but the story fails to deal with the fact that it is really the same thing. The activities of Willis and the rest of the crew are essentially masturbatory, their fantasies generated and fulfilled within their own minds with no human communication taking place. The crew, at least, recognize what they're doing for what it is. We sense that when the voyage is over, the rest of the crew will be able to resume normal relationships with women. But we cannot be sure Willis will make a similar adjustment. Willis becomes increasingly self-centered as the story progresses. He would, perhaps, be better off with a book of Shaw's. That would at least develop his imagination. As it is, the robot is better than anything Willis could possibly imagine, so Willis becomes merely a rapt listener, a voyeur. At the story's end, the space ship explodes, flinging the crewmen off into space in all directions. Willis and

Shaw drift away together, perhaps to be picked up by a rescue ship, perhaps not. Willis has, by this time, become completely selfish. He demands that the robot entertain him: "*Say* it, Mr. Shaw. . . . Say it again. . . . Please sir. . . . I want some more!"

"Downwind from Gettysburg" is centered upon an intriguing idea. A man named Booth puts a bullet through the head of a mechanical replica of Abraham Lincoln—much like the animated robot of Lincoln found at Disneyland. Booth is captured and held in the theater by security guards while Bayes, apparently the theater manager, questions him as to why he did it. Booth says the robot made him jealous—". . . jealous of anything that works right, anything that's perfect, anything that's beautiful all to itself, anything that lasts I don't care what it is!" The opportunity to examine this response to a man-like machine is there, but the story never takes advantage of it. Instead Bayes berates Booth for being a publicity hound, and declares that Booth will not be able to take advantage of what he has done. "You're a has-been that never was. And you're going to stay that way, spoiled and narcissistic and small and mean and rotten." Bayes' contempt for Booth seems based more on the affection Bayes had for the robot than on outrage at Booth's vandalism. The story also attempts to generate some sympathy for the robot's designer, Phipps. But both Phipps and Bayes have confused their feelings about Lincoln with their feelings for the robot to such an extent that Booth appears to be the healthiest of the three. The lack of clarity as to just what the robot is supposed to mean results in an ambiguous and unfocused conclusion.

"I Sing the Body Electric" is almost a commercial for robots as human substitutes. It is the story of three children whose lives are enriched by the arrival of a mechanical grandmother. Bradbury says he wrote this story to help refute the idea that all machines are bad, and much space in the story is taken up with a rather academic argument on the value of machines. The robot is of obvious enough value in replacing the children's recently deceased mother. She can eject kite-flying threads from her index finger, cook fabulous meals, recite all manner of stories from memory, and even recall on command anything a child has ever said to her, spitting it out neatly typed on a piece of paper hidden inside a freshly-baked fortune cookie. But the relationship of child to machine is one dimensional, and the story reveals, in spite of itself, the essential narcissism behind the robot-as-human fantasy. For instance, the electric grandmother alters the appearance of her face so that she resembles whatever child she is talking to. The children all come to love the robot, but is seems just as likely that a child—or any human being— might come to resent a superhuman, all-attentive, all-remembering, all-forgiving, flattering mirror-image of himself. The robot performs the two main functions of a machine to perfection: it serves and it remembers. But the story implies that these are also the functions of a grandmother.

Real grandmothers, unlike Bradbury's machine, often demand service, expect affection, require consideration and adaption to their frailties. The great failure of the robot, which the story seems to ignore, is that it demands nothing of the children, and hence offers them no escape from selfishness. The children do not learn love—the robot needs nothing so the children can give her nothing. At the story's end, the children, finally grown old, can only become selfish children again, fingering the robot's starting key in the hope she will return to tend to their needs.

MAN vs. MACHINE

Bradbury treats the difficulties and threats man can experience from machines more successfully. Robots are not the only mechanical servants which can go awry, and Bradbury has written stories about an impressive number of others. Man can be harmed by machines that are not there when they are needed. "Almost the End of the World" treats this theme in a comic manner, as the world desperately tries to fill its spare time once TV has been taken away forever. In "A Piece of Wood," a young sergeant invents a machine which will do away with another type of machine, specifically by destroying all metal used in weapons. The sergeant's superior officer is horrified at the threat of impending peace. A threat of another kind, with a more poignant resolution is found in "The Flying Machine." The scene is China in 400 A.D. The Emperor Yuan and his servant encounter a man who has made a wondrous discovery:

> In the sky, laughing so high that you could hardly hear him laugh, was a man; and the man was clothed in bright papers and reeds to make wings and a beautiful yellow tail and he was soaring all about like the largest bird in a universe of birds.

It is a flying machine, discovered ahead of its time and, as the Emperor sadly realizes, too far ahead of its time. The Emperor has what few men in history have had, absolute power to turn back the clock. The story maintains the tone of a fairy tale while detailing the tragic decision Emperor and inventor must face.

One of Bradbury's most famous machines is the children's electronic playroom in "The Veldt." The story is a chilling fable, a kind of exaggerated warning to the sort of parents who might, in an earlier age, have let their children watch too much television. Rather than stunt their imaginations as television might have done, however, the electronic playroom brings the children's fantasies to living, breathing, three-dimensional life. When the parents realize that the kids are spending too much time in the playroom, they threaten to pull the plug. But before they can accomplish this, the children conjure up an African veldt, complete with hungry lions, into which the parents are sent on a brief but fatal safari.

The ultimate solution to the problem of pesky home appliances is to be found in "The Murderer." This comic tale consists mainly of a conversation between a man and his psychiatrist. The man has become fed up with his super-mechanized house:

> It's one of those talking, singing, humming, weather-reporting, poetry-reading, novel-reciting, jingling-jangling, rockaby-crooning-when-you-go-to-bed houses. A house that screams opera to you in the shower and teaches you Spanish in your sleep.

So, he buys a gun and begins "murdering" the place:

> I ran to the kitchen, where the stove was just whining, "Turn me *over!*" In the middle of a mechanical omelet I did the stove to death. Oh, how it sizzled and screamed, "I'm shorted!" Then the telephone rang like a spoiled brat. I shoved it down the Insinkerator. I must state here and now I have *nothing* against the Insinkerator; it was an innocent bystander.

The story gives enthusiastic support to anyone who has ever been annoyed by gadgets which cause more inconvenience than they alleviate. The concept of the totally mechanized house is developed at greater length, and in a more somber tone, in the chapter "There Will Come Soft Rains" from *The Martian Chronicles*.

The ability of machinery to cause destruction at a distance is explored in "Night Call, Collect." The distance here, of course, is in time and not in space. Barton finds himself alone on Mars, and programs an elaborate series of practical jokes into the planet's automatic telephone system. Fifty years later, the phones ring, and Barton listens to the taunts of his own voice. No longer in control of the situation, he is an old man who has forgotten what he did to the phones. But the phone system is in fine shape, and it efficiently leads Barton to his death. The irony of the machine as faithful servant is absolute.

Bradbury's largest and most dangerous machine is nothing less than an entire city. "The City" has waited for 20,000 years on a lonely planet once devastated by Earthmen. When a spaceship from Earth lands again on the planet, the city is waiting to greet it. Bradbury gradually reveals the operation and purpose of the robot city. We watch as it secretly measures and tests the occupants of the spaceship to determine if these are indeed men from Earth. Then, the city suddenly and shockingly reveals itself as a terrible and complex weapon. Bradbury develops in this story what few writers about other planets have done, a true and vivid sense of "alienness." The city operates on principles utterly remote from human values. It performs an act of revenge, but in a completely abstract way, since the offender parties no longer exist and the recipients of the revenge have long since forgotten the crime.

"The Lost City of Mars" is another mechanical town, one that does not enter into combat with its visitors, but which changes them nonetheless. The city is sought by some tourists on Mars, the guests of a wealthy man who wishes to test his new yacht on a recently filled canal. The Martian name for the city is Dia-Sao, "The City of Doom." When the travelers stumble upon the city hidden under a mountain, their presence causes the great sleeping machine to come to life. The gates to the city swing open, air begins circulating, lights go on. The tourists each go their separate way, and each discovers why the city is called Doom. The problem, apparently not foreseen by its builders, is that the city is too perfect. It is a giant wish-fulfillment device which can make fantasies come true so vividly that it becomes a drug. The city exemplifies everything that is wrong with the robots in "G. B. S.— Mark V" and "I Sing the Body Electric." By stealing a person's dreams, the city in effect steals his soul. Cara Corelli, an aging beauty, discovers a "palace of mirrors."

> As she walked through a maze, the mirrors took away a day, and then a week, and then a month and then a year and then two years of time from her face.
> It was a palace of splendid and soothing lies . . .

This mirror maze echoes the more realistic maze in "The Dwarf" and the more magical maze in *Something Wicked This Way Comes*. All three mazes reflect the unfulfilled wishes of their visitors, with unfortunate consequences.

Parkhill, who has a natural bent for mechanics, finds himself "staring off down a corridor of machines that ran waiting for a solid mile of garage, shed, hoist, lift, storage bin, oil tank, and strewn shrapnel of tools glittering and ready for his grip; if he started now, he might work his way to the end of the giant's ever-constant garage, accident, collision, and repair works shed in thirty years!"

For those in the party mature enough to recognize the function of their fantasies and to not be completely absorbed by them, the city becomes a liberating experience. Harpwell, an alcoholic poet caught in continuous screaming battles with his wife, finds himself alone in a vast room. "In the middle of this room which was roughly a two-hundred-foot circle stood a device, a machine. In this machine were dials, rheostats and switches, a seat, and a steering wheel." Harpwell finds that the machine is a sort of carnival ride that allows its rider to experience violent death as often as he wishes. First Harpwell goes through a fiery car crash: "He felt himself jerked now this way and that. He was a torch hurtled skyward. His arms and legs danced a crazy rigadoon in midair as he felt his peppermint stick bones snap in brittle and agonizing ecstasies." After he has put himself through countless violent deaths, Harpwell emerges from the room a changed man. When he meets his wife, he tells her: "I won't need you any more, dead Meg, Meggy-Megan. You're free, also, like an awful conscience. Go haunt someone else, girl. Go destroy. I forgive you your sins on me, for I have at last forgiven myself."

Aaronson thinks he sees the city for what it is immediately: "no more and no less than an economy-size juke-box ravening under its idiot breath." Actually, the city is somewhat more than this. It is like a living thing, and it has been programmed for self-preservation. It knows how to lure and hold the men it needs. Those it does not need it distracts or disposes of. The self-destructive are encouraged to act upon themselves. As for the outwardly violent, "the hunter" in the party finds himself in the Museum of Weapons. He chooses a gun and begins searching for the heart of the biggest game around, the city itself. Unwittingly he plays into the city's plans and, once disposed of, allows the city to relax and shut down until the next intrusion.

"The Lost City of Mars" represents Bradbury's ultimate machine. It is the logical extension of the electric grandmother in "I Sing the Body Electric." The problem with it is succinctly stated by Wilder: "Good God . . . the place is Hell. The Martians had enough sense to get out. They saw they had overbuilt themselves. The damn city does everything, which is too much!"

ORWELLIAN TALES

Pessimists about the future of mankind have not always envisioned atomic extermination. An uncomfortable survival under a worldwide totalitarian state has also been suggested as a grim possibility. George Orwell's *1984* represents the hub of such writing, and as such it is the logical antithesis of such Utopian tales as H. G. Wells' *Things to Come*. Bradbury was never keen on Orwell's view of the future, and that attitude has intensified. Recently he has written:

> Nineteen eighty-four will never arrive. Yes, the year itself will show up but not as a Kremlin in gargoyle or an Orwellian beast. We have for the time being, anyway, knocked Big Brother into the next century. With luck and if we keep our eyes on the ballot box and our chameleon politicos, he may never return.

Nevertheless, Bradbury has written two tales of a specifically Orwellian future, "The Pedestrian," and *Fahrenheit 451*. Like many of the end-of-the-world stories discussed in Chapter 4, these works date from the early 1950s, when fears of atomic war and the Cold War were shifting into high gear.

"The Pedestrian" is one of Bradbury's most famous stories, and is a classic example of the Bradbury style of science fiction. The viewpoint is humanistic and in this case, antitechnological. The story's only character is a loner, self-exiled from his community, sensitive, and with his own set of values. He is also a writer. It is 2053, and Leonard Mead is the last man in his city who goes for walks. Everyone else stays indoors watching television. Mead is a sensualist who takes particular pleasure in the quiet of the empty streets under the moonlight. He is alive and cannot help noticing as he walks through the deserted streets that ". . . it was not unequal to walking through a graveyard where only the faintest glimmers of firefly light appeared in flickers behind the windows." In such a world, Mead is a suspicious character, and in the course of this particular walk he is stopped and questioned by a police car. There are no men in the car, it is only a robot, so Mead is in the position of defending himself to a machine:

> "Your name?" said the police car in a metallic whisper . . .
> "Leonard Mead," he said.
> "Speak up!"
> "Leonard Mead!"
> "Business or profession?"
> "I guess you'd call me a writer."
> "No profession," said the police car, as if talking to itself.

Unlike the machines which Bradbury likes, the police car has no imagination behind it, nor can it inspire any. The car picks up Mead as a suspected lunatic not because he is behaving strangely, but because his answers cannot satisfy the logic of the machine. When Mead explains simply what he is doing, the machine nearly short-circuits: "Walking, just walking, walking?" Mead admits that no one has bought any of his writing for some time because everyone is watching television. Unlike other Bradbury misfits such as the dwarf, or the old man in "To the Chicago Abyss," Mead cannot turn professional. His problem is a little like that of Marie in "The Next in Line": he is alone and alive in a city of the dead.

FAHRENHEIT 451

Fahrenheit 451 is one of only two novels Bradbury has written. The other is *Something Wicked This Way Comes.* (*Dandelion Wine* and *The Martian Chronicles* are often referred to as novels, but they are really collections of separate stories unified by theme and specially written bridge passages.) *Fahrenheit 451* is a short novel, an expansion of a story, "The Fireman," originally published in *Galaxy.* The book is about as far as Bradbury has come in the direction of using science fiction for social criticism. Actually, the premise of the book is rather farfetched—that firemen in some future state no longer fight fires but set them, having become arms of a political program aimed at stamping out all literature. This purging of the written word, particularly of the imaginative sort, is found in other stories, most strikingly in "Pillar of Fire" and "The Exiles." But in these other stories the tone is clearly that of a fantasy. *Fahrenheit 451* is realistic in tone, but keeps such a tight focus on the developing awareness of fireman Guy Montag that we can successfully overlook the improbability of his occupation. In fact, the very improbability of Montag's work allows Bradbury to maintain a certain detachment in the book, so that basic themes such as freedom of speech, the value of imagination, the authority of the state, individualism versus conformity, and so on, can be developed and explored without becoming either too realistic or too allegorical.

In the course of the book, Montag goes through what today might be called consciousness raising. He begins as a loyal fireman, burning what he is told to burn, progresses through a period of doubts and questioning, and ends up rebelling against the system and doing his part to keep man's literary heritage alive. But the bones of the plot do little to convey the feeling of the book. Bradbury's world here seems much closer to the present than the future—not so much in terms of its overall structure as in terms of its more intimate details. Some of the characterizations—Montag's wife, given over to drugs and mindless television; Clarisse, an archetypal hippie or flower child; and the old woman, who defies the firemen by pouring kerosene over her books and her own body before striking a match—might have been drawn from the turbulent political events of the sixties. It is almost necessary to remind oneself that *Fahrenheit 451* was published in 1953.

Many of Bradbury's pet themes are to be found in the novel. Metamorphosis is a major theme of the story, for in the course of it Montag changes from book-burner to living-book. Montag the fireman is intensely aware of the power of fire: "It was a special pleasure to see things eaten, to see things blackened and *changed*." He himself is changed every time he goes out on a job: "He knew that when he returned to the firehouse, he might wink at himself, a minstrel man, burnt-corked, in the mirror."

Machines are of crucial importance. Overall, the book traces Montag's flight from the dangerous mechanical world of the city to the traditional haven of the country. Montag at first feels comfortable with machines, especially his flame-throwing equipment. The first time Montag meets Clarisse he views the scene in mechanical terms: "The autumn leaves blew over the moonlit pavement in such a way as to make the girl who was moving there seem fixed to a gliding walk, letting the motion of the wind and leaves carry her forward." But many mechanical things are repellent to Montag, particularly the equipment the medical technicians use on his wife after she has taken an overdose of sleeping pills: "They had two machines, really. One of them slid down your stomach like a black cobra down an echoing well looking for all the old water and the old time gathered there."

Montag's particular mechanical enemy is the fire station's Mechanical Hound, more like a huge spider, actually, with its "bits of ruby glass and . . . sensitive capillary hairs in the Nylon-brushed nostrils . . . that quivered gently, gently, its eight legs spidered under it on rubber-padded paws." As Montag becomes more fascinated with books and nearer to betrayal of his duties as a fireman, the hound becomes more suspicious of him. The hound is then symbolic of the relentless, heartless pursuit of the State.

When Montag finally flees the city, he must first cross a mechanical moat, a highway 100 yards across on which the "beetle" cars seem to take pleasure in using pedestrians for target practice. Other machines Montag grows to hate are the radio and television that reduce their audience, Montag's wife, for one, into listless zombies.

But *Fahrenheit 451* is not primarily a work of social criticism. Its antimachine and antiwar elements are there primarily as background for Montag's spiritual development. It is interesting that this development seems to be in the direction of social outcast. Granted that Montag's society has its evils, but at the end of the book we are not so sure that Montag will be completely happy with his new-found friends, the book people. What we are sure of it that Montag has entrenched himself as nay-sayer to a society that has become hostile and destructive toward the past. Montag joins the book people whose task, as Granger puts it, is "remembering." But even as he does so, he promises himself that he will one day follow the refugees from the bombed-out city, seeking, though this is not stated, perhaps his wife, perhaps Clarisse. Most of the book people are like the old man in "To the Chicago Abyss," essentially harmless, using their talents for remembering things to aid their society in whatever way they can. But Montag may perhaps be too rigid an idealist, having rejected his former society with the same vehemence as he once embraced it. Like Spender in *The Martian Chronicles*, Montag has committed murder to maintain his freedom and the integrity of his vision. Unlike Spender, but like many of Bradbury's other outsiders and misfits, Montag has successfully achieved a truce or stalemate with a world hostile to his individuality. At the end of *Fahrenheit 451*, Montag's future can go either way; toward reintegration with a new, less hostile society, or toward a continuing, perpetual alienation.

DONALD WATT

Burning Bright: Fahrenheit 451 *as Symbolic Dystopia*

"It was a pleasure to burn," begins Bradbury's *Fahrenheit 451*. "It was a special pleasure to see things eaten, to see things blackened and *changed*." In the decade following Nagasaki and Hiroshima, Bradbury's eye-catching opening for his dystopian novel assumes particular significance. America's nuclear climax to World War II signalled the start of a new age in which the awesome powers of technology, with its alarming dangers, would provoke fresh inquiries into the dimensions of man's potentiality and the scope of his brutality. *Fahrenheit 451* coincides in time and, to a degree, in temperament with Jackson Pollock's tense post-Hiroshima experiments with cobalt and cadmium red, as well as the aggressive primordial grotesques of Seymour Lipton's 1948 New York exhibition—*Moloch, Dissonance, Wild Earth, Mother.* Montag's Nero complex is especially striking in the context of the looming threat of global ruin in the postwar era: "With the brass nozzle in his fists, with this great python spitting its venomous kerosene upon the world, the blood pounded in his head, and his hands were the hands of some amazing conductor playing all the symphonies of blazing and burning to bring down the tatters and charcoal ruins of history." Montag's intense pleasure in burning somehow involves a terrible, sado-masochistic temptation to torch the globe, to blacken and disintegrate the human heritage. As Erich Fromm observes, destructiveness "is the outcome of unlived life." Modern man

From *Ray Bradbury.* © 1980 by Taplinger Publishing Co.

21

actively pursues destructiveness in order to compensate for a loss of responsibility for his future. Seeking escape from the new freedom he enjoys as a
benefit of his new technology, man is all too likely to succumb to a Dr.
Strangelove impulse to destroy himself with the very tools that gave him
freedom. The opening paragraph of Bradbury's novel immediately evokes
the consequences of unharnessed technology and contemporary man's
contented refusal to acknowledge these consequences.

In short, *Fahrenheit 451* (1953) raises the question posed by a number
of contemporary anti-utopian novels. In one way or another, Huxley's *Ape
and Essence* (1948), Orwell's *Nineteen Eighty-Four* (1948), Vonnegut's *Player
Piano* (1952), Miller's *A Canticle for Leibowitz* (1959), Hartley's *Facial Justice*
(1960), and Burgess's *A Clockwork Orange* (1962) all address themselves to the
issue of technology's impact on the destiny of man. In this sense, Mark R.
Hillegas is right in labeling *Fahrenheit 451* "almost the archetypal anti-utopia
of the new era in which we live." Whether, what, and how to burn in Bradbury's book are the issues—as implicit to a grasp of our age as electricity—
which occupy the center of the contemporary mind.

What is distinctive about *Fahrenheit 451* as a work of literature, then, is
not what Bradbury says but how he says it. With Arthur C. Clarke, Bradbury
is among the most poetic of science fiction writers. Bradbury's evocative,
lyrical style charges *Fahrenheit 451* with a sense of mystery and connotative
depth that go beyond the normal boundaries of dystopian fiction. Less
charming, perhaps, than *The Martian Chronicles*, *Fahrenheit 451* is also less
brittle. More to the point, in *Fahrenheit 451* Bradbury has created a pattern
of symbols that richly convey the intricacy of his central theme. Involved in
Bradbury's burning is the overwhelming problem of modern science: as
man's shining inventive intellect sheds more and more light on the truths of
the universe, the increased knowledge he thereby acquires, if abused, can
ever more easily fry his planet to a cinder. Burning as constructive energy,
and burning as apocalyptic catastrophe, are the symbolic poles of Bradbury's novel. Ultimately, the book probes in symbolic terms the puzzling,
divisive nature of man as a creative/destructive creature. *Fahrenheit 451*
thus becomes a book which injects originality into a literary subgenre that
can grow worn and hackneyed. It is the only major symbolic dystopia of
our time.

The plot of *Fahrenheit 451* is simple enough. In Bradbury's future, Guy
Montag is a fireman whose job it is to burn books and, accordingly,
discourage the citizenry from thinking about anything except four-wall television. He meets a young woman whose curiosity and love of natural life stir
dissatisfaction with his role in society. He begins to read books and to rebel
against the facade of diversions used to seal the masses away from the reali-

ties of personal insecurity, officially condoned violence, and periodic nuclear war. He turns against the authorities in a rash and unpremeditated act of murder, flees their lethal hunting party, and escapes to the country. At the end of the book he joins a group of self-exiled book-lovers who hope to preserve the great works of the world despite the opposition of the masses and a nuclear war against an unspecified enemy.

In such bare detail, the novel seems unexciting, even a trifle inane. But Bradbury gives his story impact and imaginative focus by means of symbolic fire. Appropriately, fire is Montag's world, his reality. Bradbury's narrative portrays events as Montag sees them, and it is natural to Montag's way of seeing to regard his experiences in terms of fire. This is a happy and fruitful arrangement by Bradbury, for he is thereby able to fuse character development, setting, and theme into a whole. Bradbury's symbolic fire gives unity, as well as stimulating depth, to *Fahrenheit 451*.

Bradbury dramatizes Montag's development by showing the interactions between his hero and other characters in the book; the way Bradbury plays with reflections of fire in these encounters constantly sheds light on key events. Clarisse, Mildred, the old woman, Beatty, Faber, and Granger are the major influences on Montag as he struggles to understand his world. The figure of Clarisse is, of course, catalytic; she is dominant in Montag's growth to awareness. The three sections into which Bradbury divides the novel are, however, most clearly organized around the leading male characters—Beatty in Part One, Faber in Part Two, and Montag himself (with Granger) in Part Three. Beatty and Faber—the one representing the annihilating function of fire, the other representing the quiet, nourishing flame of the independent creative imagination—are the poles between which Montag must find his identity, with Mildred and Clarisse reflecting the same polar opposition on another level. The men are the intellectual and didactic forces at work on Montag, while the women are the intuitive and experiential forces. Beatty articulates the system's point of view, but Mildred lives it. Faber articulates the opposition's point of view, but Clarisse lives it. Fire, color, light, darkness, and variations thereof suffuse Bradbury's account of the interplay among his characters, suggesting more subtly than straight dialogue or description the full meaning of *Fahrenheit 451*.

A closer look at each of these three sections shows just how pervasive fire is in the narrative. Part One, provocatively entitled "The Hearth and the Salamander," presents crucial incidents which prod Montag out of the hypnotic daze of his fireman's existence. His meeting with Clarisse teaches him to be aware of life—or the lack of it—around him. His wife's brush with death, and the way she is saved, exposes for Montag the pitiable state of individual existence in their society. The stunning experience with the old woman at 11 North Elm demonstrates for Montag the possibility of defiance and the power of books. By the end of the section Montag's fireman foundations have been so rudely shaken that he wonders if "maybe it would be best if the firemen themselves were burnt."

Montag's initial encounter with Clarisse illustrates the care with which Bradbury arranges his narrative. To return to the opening paragraph, Bradbury writes that the "gorging fire" Montag ignites "burned the evening sky red and yellow and black." Even the wind has "turned dark with burning." Here Bradbury establishes two important aspects of Montag's destructive burning: it is blackening, not enlightening; and it poses a threat to nature. Clarisse provides a contrast to each of these aspects. Montag is singed and blackened by his own flames, "a minstrel man, burnt-corked, in the mirror." His darkness represents the nullity, the ignorance, the vacuity of his mind, rendered blank by that burning which relieves him of responsibility. He walks home afterwards, "thinking little at all about nothing in particular." In contrast, Bradbury carefully stresses Clarisse's whiteness. Her dress is white, her face "slender and milk-white" and "bright as snow in the moonlight." White—the presence of all color—confronts dark—the absence of all color—when Clarisse and Montag meet. Montag, unsettled by Clarisse's desire to slow down and observe what happens to people, tells her: "You think too many things." His mind is circumscribed and oppressed by his black beetle-colored helmet, a symbol of his nonthinking commitment to Beatty's authority. But Clarisse's face reminds him of the luminous dial of a clock in a dark room at midnight, "with a white silence and a glowing, all certainty and knowing what it has to tell of the night passing swiftly on toward further darkness, but moving also toward a new sun." In figurative language evoking some of his major symbolism, Bradbury foreshadows the rest of the novel. Clarisse will remain with Montag in spirit even after she disappears, to illuminate his way through the dark night of his ordeal and bring him to a realization of the possibility of a new dawn for mankind with Granger's dissident group.

The meeting with Clarisse also introduces a contrast in Bradbury's narrative between the grimy, harsh, destructive milieu of the firemen and the clean, regenerative world of nature. Montag can never entirely wash away the smell of kerosene which, he tells Clarisse, "is nothing but perfume to me." With her, though, he cannot help but notice "the faintest breath of fresh apricots and strawberries in the air." Montag's firehouse environment glitters with the artificial light of brass and silver. The men's faces are burned, not by the sun but "by a thousand real and ten thousand imaginary fires, whose work flushed their cheeks and fevered their eyes." Bradbury identifies them with their platinum igniter flames; they smoke "eternally burning black pipes." Their hair is charcoal, their brows soot-covered, their cheeks the color of smeared blue ash. Montag sees these men as images of himself and is appalled by the correlation between their roles and their appearances, by the "color of cinders and ash about them, and the continual smell of burning from their pipes." Conversely, Clarisse brings Montag emblems from nature—autumn leaves, flowers, chestnuts. She appreciates the way old leaves smell like cinnamon. She uses a dandelion to rub on her chin and Montag's as a test of whether they love anyone. Her connection with the smells and objects of nature is another way in which Bradbury anticipates the ending of his book, when Montag revels in the refreshing odors of the countryside. Montag's growth is, in one sense, a journey, both physical and psychological, away from the mechanized, conformist environment of the firehouse, with the men playing an interminable card game, to the natural setting of the woods, where men dwell on the best that has ever been thought or said.

Against Montag's fierce, tight, fiery grin, Bradbury juxtaposes Clarisse's soft inner warmth. Hers is a gentle flame which promises more light to Montag than the inferno of the firemen: "Her face, turned to him now, was fragile milk crystal with a soft and constant light in it. It was not the hysterical light of electricity but—what? But the strangely comfortable and rare and gently flattering light of the candle." The thought reminds Montag of an incident in his childhood when, during a power failure, he and his mother lit one last candle and discovered "such illumination" in their quiet silence that they did not want the power to return too quickly. The figure of Clarisse glowing gently as a candle—slender, soft, serene—provides a marked contrast to the voracious acts of arson committed by the firemen. Montag thinks she is like a mirror "that refracted your own light to you." In his experience people were "more often—he searched for a simile, found one in his work—torches, blazing away until they whiffed out." In Montag's high-tension society, people burn themselves out from the inside, consumed by the ordained violence and mindless distractions certified by the authorities.

He searched for a simile, found one in his work. The appropriateness of Bradbury's symbolism consists of its logical derivation from Montag's perceptions, from his orientation and habits as a fireman. It is significant that Montag associates the fireman's job of burning with a process of darkening. Gradually he comes to see darkness as a revealing feature of his benighted society. Clarisse's uncle's house is brightly lit late at night, "while all the other houses were kept to themselves in darkness." Black jets tear across the night sky, sounding as if they will pulverize the stars. The omnipresent dark is an emblem of their age, the menacing jets symbols of the approaching doom of civilization. The Mechanical Hound, lurking in "a dark corner of the firehouse," is a fitting representative of unrelenting pursuit and execution for those who seek to shed some light on their age.

When Montag enters his bedroom after his disturbing first conversation with Clarisse, he finds: "Complete darkness, not a hint of the silver world outside, the windows tightly shut, the chamber a tomb-world where no sound from the great city could penetrate." The darkness here is that of the mausoleum, the deathly milieu of the TV "family" and the thimble ear radio, in which Mildred entombs herself. Sharply juxtaposed to Clarisse, Mildred takes on the coldness of a corpse. Bradbury conveys his meaning by a return to a simile Montag has just discovered: "He felt his smile slide away, melt, fold over and down on itself like a tallow skin, like the stuff of a fantastic candle burning too long and now collapsing and now blown out. Darkness. He was not happy." The darkness of Montag's gloomy home life closes over him as, in the suffocating atmosphere, he makes his way "toward his open, separate, and therefore cold bed." Soon he sees that Mildred has unwittingly taken thirty sleeping capsules. One senses that she would hardly be less frigid and no more alive than she is as an incipient cadaver. The mechanics from the emergency hospital bring machines to pump out her stomach:

> One of them slid down into your stomach like a black cobra down an echoing well looking for all the old water and the old time gathered there. It drank up the green matter that flowed to the top in a slow boil. Did it drink of the darkness? Did it suck out all the poisons accumulated with the years?

The handymen distress Montag by the impersonal way in which they replace Mildred's vital juices. But the operation is now so common, the disease so widespread, that they can handle nine or ten calls per night. The implication is clear: Mildred is no special case. The poisonous darkness within her has become endemic to their way of life. The darkness suggests all the unimagined psychic bile that builds up in people, to embitter them, alienate them from one another, snuff out any inner light on their mode of existing.

Bradbury's symbolic language pervades and animates the first few scenes of *Fahrenheit 451*. The result is the creation of a mood or an aura about Montag's thoughts and experiences. The many passing strokes, hints, and suggestions of what is shaping Montag's mind—his many graphic responses in his own terms to experiences which are to him evocative, sometimes intangible and bewildering—are the key to Bradbury's distinctive style. Bradbury's figurative evocations bring the reader to the threshold of Montag's inner self, "that other self, the subconscious idiot that ran babbling at times, quite independent of will, habit, and conscience." In Bradbury's opening pages the reader can detect, through the symbols which Montag draws out of his surroundings, a dawning awareness of his real psychic being pulsing beneath the rubble of his society. Bradbury has meticulously selected his symbols at the beginning of the book, for he will return to them and develop them to give *Fahrenheit 451* inner coherence, unity, and depth of meaning.

The old woman at 11 North Elm, for example, startles Montag by quoting Hugh Latimer's famous words to Nicholas Ridley as they were being burned alive for their unorthodox views in the sixteenth century: "we shall this day light such a candle, by God's grace, in England, as I trust shall never be put out." Like Latimer and Ridley, the old woman burns to death rather than sacrifice her views, her books. The Oxford heretics being burned at the stake were a flame whose light has not been extinguished since. Montag soon tells Mildred that the fire which killed the old woman smolders inside him and will "last me the rest of my life." As the firemen chop away at the old woman's house, Montag thinks this a particularly difficult assignment: "Always before it had been like snuffing a candle." Usually the victims are taken away before their houses are put to the torch. But the old woman proudly defies the firemen and burns along with her books. She becomes a candle that perseveres and shines like a beacon in Montag's mind. One cannot help but associate her with Clarisse.

Beatty's visit to Montag's home, where he explains the rationale behind burning books for the good of society, is the culmination of Part One. Beatty's ever-present pipe is a symbol of his commitment to a life of burning. His face, with its phosphorescent cheeks, is ruddy from his proximity to flames. Like the iron dragon that transports his crew to their victims' houses, Beatty is always puffing forth great clouds of smoke. He constantly plays with "his eternal matchbox," which guarantees "one million lights in this igniter." Obsessed, Beatty strikes "the chemical match abstractedly, blow out, strike, blow out, strike, speak a few words, blow out. He looked at the flame. He blew, he looked at the smoke." Beatty is a salamander man, at home in fire and smoke. As such, he is admirably suited to tell Montag about the beauty of burning:

> "Colored people don't like *Little Black Sambo*. Burn it. White people don't feel good about *Uncle Tom's Cabin*. Burn it. Someone's written a book on tobacco and cancer of the lungs? The cigarette people are weeping? Burn the book. Serenity, Montag. Peace, Montag. Take your fight outside. Better yet, into the incinerator. Funerals are unhappy and pagan? Eliminate them, too. Five minutes after a person is dead he's on his way to

the Big Flue, the Incinerators serviced by helicopters all over the country. Ten minutes after death a man's a speck of black dust. Let's not quibble over individuals with memoriams. Forget them. Burn all, burn everything. Fire is bright and fire is clean."

Beatty contends that the glory of fire is that it eliminates controversy, discontent, and unhappiness. In their society, people are fed "non-combustible data," not philosophy or sociology. The firemen, he says, "stand against the small tide of those who want to make everyone unhappy with conflicting theory and thought." Curiously invoking the specter of fire's natural enemy, water, Beatty urges the importance of maintaining the firemen's approach to existence: "Don't let the torrent of melancholy and drear philosophy drown our world." Beatty warns Montag to hold back the flood of confusing ideas which would put out the firemen's simplifying torch. Actually what is happening within Montag is the birth of another kind of fire, a kindling of his awareness of individual responsibility. Beatty's burning sears the responsibility out of the individual's life. But Clarisse has told Montag that she and her uncle believe in responsibility, and Montag is beginning to recognize that a person is behind each of the books he has burned as a fireman.

The meaning of the title, "The Hearth and the Salamander," for Part One now becomes clear. On one hand, the hearth evokes the warmth and friendliness of a good book by the fireside. By the hearth one silently explores, like Clarisse, without bias or haste, the meaning of experience. The hearth also suggests the heat of emotional and intellectual stimulation drawn by the reader from the creative fire of the writer. Montag's instinct is for the hearth, as he sits in his hall through a rainy November afternoon poring through the books he has hidden in the ventilator of the air conditioner. The salamander, on the other hand, is Beatty's preference; it is an emblem of the firemen. Unlike the hearth-dweller, the salamander does not sit next to the fire, but in it. Of course, salamanders can survive in fire; but Bradbury's point is that men are not salamanders. When immersed in fire, men are destroyed. If fire is viewed as Bradbury's emblem for technology, the message becomes obvious.

The inner flame kindled in Montag by Clarisse and the old woman flares up in Part Two, as Montag comes under the illuminating influence of Faber. Bradbury links Faber with Clarisse by the dominant whiteness which Montag notices about the old man when he visits him at his home: "The old man looked as if he had not been out of the house in years. He and the white plaster walls inside were much the same. There was white in the flesh of his mouth and his cheeks and his hair was white and his eyes had faded, with white in the vague blueness there." Bradbury also associates Faber with nature and natural smells. Montag is haunted by the memory of his original meeting with Faber in a green park; now Faber, in his house, reflects aloud that books "smell like nutmeg or some spice from a foreign land."

Bradbury develops Faber's position and impact on Montag by extending the applications of the novel's major symbol. As if in response to what Beatty says at the close of Part One, Faber tells Montag his view of their society's way of life: "They don't know that this is all one huge big blazing meteor that makes a pretty fire in space, but that someday it'll have to *hit*. They see only the blaze, the pretty fire, as you saw it." For Faber, the firemen's philosophy of eradicating knowledge for the contentment of the masses is merely a joyride of irresponsibility and evasion that is bound to end in a colossal smashup. Faber likes Montag's idea of planting books in firemen's houses and turning in the alarm: "To see the firehouses burn across the land, destroyed as hotbeds of treason. The salamander devours his tail!" Faber sees, too, that their basic hope should be a remolding of the entire society: "The whole culture's shot through. The skeleton needs melting and reshaping." There is dramatic irony in Faber's words. As Montag leaves him with the ear radio intact (for them to keep in touch), the night feels as if "the sky might fall upon the city and turn it to chalk dust, and the moon go up in red fire." Bradbury's foreshadowing of the cataclysm that befalls their society at the book's end is another example of how his variations on fire contribute coherence to the narrative.

Bradbury also extends his notion, introduced by Mildred's overdose of sleeping pills, that Montag's society is consuming and burying itself in fits of angst. Bradbury likens the wild colors, savage music, and canned entertainment spewing without end out of the multiwalled TV parlor to "an eruption of Vesuvius." Mrs. Bowles and Mrs. Phelps arrive at Montag's house to watch the White Clowns. With their "Cheshire Cat smiles burning through the walls of the house," they vanish "into the volcano's mouth." Bradbury's figure conveys a sense of the ladies' immersion in a wash of lava; they are already buried alive, like the citizens of Pompeii, under the ashes of the volcano that contains them. After Montag interrupts their programs, they sit in the parlor smoking cigarettes and "examining their blazing fingernails as if they had caught fire from his look." Representatives of all the masses living under the torch of organized violence and ever-impending war, the women are "burning with tension. Any moment they might hiss a long sputtering hiss and explode." Montag mercilessly exposes the ingrained fear, guilt, and anxiety with which they live and from which "the relatives" can only partially distract them. As Montag prepares to read Matthew Arnold's *Dover Beach*, the room is "blazing hot," he feverishly feels at once "all fire" and "all coldness," and the women wait "in the middle of an empty desert," sitting "in the great hot emptiness." Bradbury's symbolism is hard at work. Deprived of the White Clowns, the women feel abandoned as on a desert. On a desert there is no escape from the fiery sun—the scathing truths conveyed by Arnold's poem. In the reading, *Dover Beach* explodes through the veneers of superficiality protecting the women and confirms Montag's thought that the books in his house are dynamite which Mildred tries to disperse "stick by stick." Montag's angry outburst against Mrs. Bowles' protests releases some of his own pent-up heat. His rage is his first real spark of rebellion, and it soon fans into a hotter outburst against the unfortunate Beatty.

Faber finds himself stimulated by Montag's spirited words, but he warns Montag to allow "a little of my cowardice to be distilled in you tonight." Faber cautions Montag to temper and control his heat with some cold discretion. By Faber's cowardice, Bradbury means prudence cultivated over a lifetime. Faber's advice, in effect, develops water as a useful, diversified part of Bradbury's symbolism. When he talks with Faber earlier, Montag says he will need help to handle Beatty: "I need an umbrella to keep off the rain. I'm so damned afraid I'll drown if he gets me again." The suggestion here is that Montag does not want the freshly created fire of his inner being to be deluged by the neutralizing, superficial arguments of his fire chief. This complication of Bradbury's figure may be confusing. Beatty fears water as an agent hostile to his fiery environment; Faber urges Montag to cool his rebellious fire; and Montag does not want to dampen the spark of insight he has achieved. Part of the power of symbolism is its ability to assume different, even contradictory, meanings in variations on the same theme. The deeper meaning of Bradbury's fire and water seems to be that the firemen's fire, in its negativity, is meant to put out any flame of inspiration or disagreement or creativity on the part of the individual. In its profoundest sense, the mission of Beatty's crew is to extinguish fires by burning them.

A less subtle mixture of fire and water occurs in *Fahrenheit 451* when Montag goes downtown after the poetry reading. On his way to the firehouse, he reflects that there are two people inside him—the ignorant fool, Montag, and the old man talking to him through the ear transmitter:

> In the days to follow, and in the nights when there was no moon and in the nights when there was a very bright moon shining on the earth, the old man would go on with this talking and this talking, drop by drop, stone by stone, flake by flake. His mind would well over at last and he would not be Montag any more, this old man told him, assured him, promised him. He would be Montag-plus-Faber, fire plus water, and then, one day, after everything had mixed and simmered and worked away in silence, there would be neither fire nor water, but wine.

Earlier, Clarisse objects that the authorities told them that their society's hectic deluge of group activities was "wine when it's not." Her words, which have stuck in Montag's mind, provide him with a sensual, appropriate figure to explain what he believes is happening to himself. Montag sees his own fiery youth being matured—fermented—by the life experiences of Faber. The water that is linked with Faber suggests the vital flow of his hopes for man. This water somehow merges with the river of life on which Montag floats in his escape from the Mechanical Hound. Out of the metaphoric blending of Montag's fire and Faber's water, Montag envisions the emersion of a pleasing, stimulating, fresh psychic substance—represented as a vintage yield of wine.

Bradbury continues to play variations on burning in the final sequence of Part Two, where the two different, indeed opposite, kinds of flame flicker out at each other. Montag's return to the firehouse provokes Beatty to welcome him: "I hope you'll be staying with us, now that your fever is done and your sickness over." For Beatty, Montag's inner burning is the result of a fever. From Beatty's point of view, this burning means that a man has been unwell. But Montag wishes to nourish the burning; he doesn't want to return to normal. Beatty, however, enervates Montag with his "alcohol-flame stare" and a confusing barrage of conflicting quotations. Montag feels he cannot go on burning with the firemen, yet he is as powerless to answer Beatty's onslaught as he would be to stop the Salamander, the fire engine, that "gaseous dragon roaring to life." Montag is chagrined by the recollection of reading a book to "the chaff women in his parlor tonight" and realizes it was as senseless as "trying to put out fires with waterpistols." In his typically figurative way, Bradbury is telling us that Montag's psychic temperature cannot remotely approach the 451 degrees Fahrenheit which is the minimal level of power enjoyed by the firemen. On appearance, at any rate, and for the moment, Montag's rage for individual responsibility is puny by comparison with the firepower of Beatty's crew.

The ramifications of Bradbury's two fires become clearer in Part Three, "Burning Bright," for the sequence of events portrays Montag's movement from one to the other, from the gorging arson of his own house to the comforting campfire of Granger. In this section Montag's growth develops into a belief in what Blake symbolizes in his poem, "The Tiger":

> Tiger! Tiger! Burning bright
> In the forests of the night,
> What immortal hand or eye
> Could frame thy fearful symmetry?

Blake's tiger is the generative force of the human imagination, the creative/destructive force which for him is the heart of man's complex nature. Montag becomes Bradbury's tiger in the forests of the night. He becomes a hunted outcast from an overly tame society by making good his violent escape from the restraining cage of the city. In his rebellion and flight, Montag *is* burning bright. Paradoxically, the flame of his suppressed human spirit spreads through his whole being after his horrible murder of Beatty. In burning Beatty, Montag shares the ambivalence of Blake's tiger, with its symbolic combination of wrath and beauty, its "fearful symmetry."

Bradbury introduces another allusion, one connected with his major symbol, when the fire engine pulls up before Montag's house at the opening of the third section and Beatty chides him: "Old Montag wanted to fly near the sun and now that he's burnt his wings, he wonders why." Beatty's reference is to the mythological Icarus who soared into the sky with Dedalus, his father, on wax wings. But Icarus, carried away by the joy of flying, went too close to the sun, causing his wings to melt and making him fall. Clarisse, we recall, used to stay up nights waiting for the sunrise, and her face reminded Montag of a clock dial pointing toward a new sun. The sun, traditional symbol of truth and enlightenment, is antithetical to the dark night of ignorance that Beatty spreads across the land. The difference between Montag and Icarus—which, of course, Beatty will never live to see—is that Montag, though crippled by the Mechanical Hound, survives his own daring. Burning bright and living dangerously, Montag skirts the destruction Beatty plans for him and flees to the liberated periphery of society where pockets of truth endure undimmed.

At the beginning of Part Three, however, Beatty prevails. Montag once more enjoys the purging power of the fireman as he lays waste to his own house: "And as before, it was good to burn, he felt himself gush out in the fire, snatch, rend, rip in half with flame, and put away the senseless problem. . . . Fire was best for everything!" Montag destroys his house piecemeal, surprised that his twin beds go up "with more heat and passion and light than he would have supposed them to contain." Bradbury's lyrical style conveys Montag's fascination with the splendor and the transforming power of the flames. His books "leapt and danced like roasted birds, their wings ablaze with red and yellow feathers." He gives the TV parlor "a gift of one huge bright yellow flower of burning." Beatty affects Montag strongly with his enticing argument for burning:

> What is fire? It's a mystery. Scientists give us gobbledegook about friction and molecules. But they don't really know. Its real beauty is that it destroys responsibility and consequences. A problem gets too burdensome, then into the furnace with it. Now, Montag, you're a burden. And fire will lift you off my

shoulders, clean, quick, sure; nothing to rot later. Anti-biotic, aesthetic, practical.

With a happy vengeance Montag levels the house where he has become a stranger to his own wife. He feels as though a fiery earthquake is razing his old life as Montag the fireman, burying his artificial societal self, while in his mind his other self is running, "leaving this dead soot-covered body to sway in front of another raving fool." Beatty cannot understand that at this point Montag is inwardly turning the flamethrower against its owners, that by burning his house he is deliberately destroying his niche in Beatty's system.

Only when Beatty threatens to trace Faber does Montag realize that the logical end to his action must be the torching of his chief. As Montag recognizes, the problem is, "we never burned *right*. . . ." The shrieking, melting, sizzling body of Beatty is Bradbury's horrible emblem of the end result of a civilization based on irresponsibility. Beatty has always told Montag not to face a problem, but to burn it. Montag considers: "Well, now I've done both." One may conclude that Montag fights fire with fire.

The remainder of the novel consists of Montag's escape from the domain of the Mechanical Hound, his immersion in the countryside, and his discovery of Granger's group of bookish outcasts. Montag is still very much in Beatty's world as he flees through the city. Stung by the Mechanical Hound, his leg is "like a chunk of burnt pinelog he was carrying along as a penance for some obscure sin." As he runs his lungs feel "like burning brooms in his chest," his throat like "burnt rust." In his narrow escape from a police car, the lights from the highway lamps seem "as bright and revealing as the midday sun and just as hot," and the car bearing down on him is "a torch hurtling upon him." Montag wants to get out of the distressing heat of Beatty's city and into the cool seclusion of the country. Bradbury stresses that the real insanity of the firemen's world is the pleasure people take in random violence and destruction. Accordingly, just before he sets off to elude the Mechanical Hound, Montag tells Faber that in his death scene he would like to say just one or two words "that would sear all their faces and wake them up." He deeply regrets what he did to Beatty, transformed now into "nothing but a frame skeleton strung with asphalt tendons," but he feels he must remember, "burn them or they'll burn you. . . . Right now it's as simple as that." It is perhaps instructive to note that one of Montag's last acts in the city is to frame the fireman named Black.

Bradbury broadens Montag's perspective on burning when Montag wades into a river and floats downstream away from the harsh glare of the pursuing searchlights. The life-saving river, a symbol of life's journey and its baptismal vitality, carries Montag into the world of nature: "For the first time in a dozen years the stars were coming out above him, in great processions of wheeling fire. He saw a great juggernaut of stars form in the sky and threaten to roll over and crush him." The great fires of the cosmos have been concealed from Montag by the glittering arcs of the city. Immersed in the river and free of the electric jitters of city life, Montag at last discovers leisure to think for himself. Beatty had said that one of fire's attractions for man is its semblance of perpetual motion. Montag, reflecting on the moon's light, becomes aware that the sun burns every day, burns time, burns away the years and people's lives. Before long, he knows "why he must never burn again in his life." He sees that "if *he* burnt things with the firemen and the sun burnt Time, that meant that *everything* burned!" But he feels that somehow conserving must balance consuming:

> One of them had to stop burning. The sun wouldn't, certainly. So it looked as if it had to be Montag and the people he had worked with until a few short hours ago. Somewhere the saving and putting away had to begin again and someone had to do the saving and keeping, one way or another, in books, in records, in people's heads, any way at all so long as it was safe, free from moths, silver-fish, rust and dry-rot, and men with matches. The world was full of burning of all types and sizes. Now the guild of the asbestos-weaver must open shop very soon.

This key passage illuminates Montag's sensed need for some form of permanence to counteract the instability of destruction and change. Man should not capitulate to the tyranny of the nitrogen cycle, to the mutability characteristic of the physical, dynamic world. Montag's emerging desire is for something enduring in man's existence—history, heritage, culture. Montag seeks, in essence, a definition and a preservation of the identity of human kind.

Montag's recognition of another mode of burning, therefore, is at this stage eminently appropriate to Bradbury's theme. Enchanted by the warmth of the country, which is implicitly contrasted with the coldness of Mildred's bedroom, reminded of Clarisse by all the natural smells of the vegetation surrounding him—"a dry river smelling of hot cloves," "a smell like a cut potato from all the land," "a faint yellow odor like parsley on the table at home," "a smell like carnations from the yard [Clarisse's] next door"— Montag comes upon a campfire which strikes him as strange "because it meant a different thing to him." The difference is, he abruptly notices: "It was not burning, it was *warming*." Men hold their hands toward this warmth; they do not recoil in terror from it. Montag "hadn't known fire could look this way. He had never thought in his life that it could give as well as take. Even its smell was different." Montag feels like some forest creature "of fur and muzzle and hoof" attracted to the fire and "listening to the warm crackle of the flames." No longer a fierce tiger because he has escaped the mad jungle of Beatty's city, Montag is now like a shy, wondering animal of the woods. Free of the ceaseless noise of "the family," Montag feels the silence as well as the flame of the camp is different. The men around the fire have time to "look at the world and turn it over with the eyes, as if it were held to the center of the bonfire, a piece of steel these men were all shaping." Bradbury's figure is of utmost importance, since it recalls Faber's comment that all of civilization must be melted down and reshaped. Involved in Montag's sighting of Granger's group is the hope that the new kind of burning may bring about some possibility of a new kind of world.

The purpose of their group, Granger explains, is to preserve man's cultural heritage through the current dark age of his history. They are keepers of the flame of man's wisdom and creativity. They live in the forests of the night, harboring their gentle light against the annihilating torches of the city's firemen. But Montag, expecting "their faces to burn and glitter with the knowledge they carried, to glow as lanterns glow, with the light in them," is disappointed. There is no inner glow to their faces, only resignation. These men are now waiting for "the end of the party and the blowing out of the lamps." They know that nuclear war is imminent, that the joyride of Beatty's society is over, that the future of man is unsure: "They weren't at all certain that the things they carried in their heads might make every future dawn glow with a purer light. . . ." Shortly, the bombs turn the city into what Granger describes as "a heap of baking powder," with Mildred and the others now literally buried under the volcano in which they have burned away their existences. The contrast between fire as holocaust and fire as hearth becomes pointed as Granger's men settle around a campfire to cook bacon. Fire, like technology and knowledge, is good or bad, depending on how one uses it.

At the close, Granger compares man with the Phoenix, the mythical bird that lives for hundreds of years in the desert, consumes itself in fire, and then rises reborn from its own ashes. It appears to Granger that man periodically does the same thing, with the difference that man knows what he is doing to himself: "We know all the damn silly things we've done for a thousand years and as long as we know that and always have it around where we can see it, some day we'll stop making the goddam funeral pyres and jumping in the middle of them." Granger hopes that, with more people each generation seeing man's record of folly, some day they will "remember so much that we'll build the biggest steamshovel in history and dig the biggest grave of all time and shove war in and cover it up." Bradbury's mood at best is one of modified optimism, at worst, skeptical ambivalence. The question he raises but leaves unexplored is whether man can ever transcend the cycles of construction and devastation that have characterized his history. Granger's hope notwithstanding, one must remember the phoenix-disc is also one of the firemen's symbols.

Yet at the very end, Bradbury does inject the promise of at least a seasonal renewal, and perhaps more, for man. As the men put out their campfire, "the day was brightening all about them as if a pink lamp had been given more wick." The candle figure is instructive, for it brings the reader all the way back to Clarisse and the kind, humane light she stands for. As they break camp the men, including Granger, fall in behind Montag, suggesting that he will become their leader. Montag, which means Monday in German, will conceivably light their way to a fresh beginning for man. As he wonders what he can say to make their trip upriver a little easier, Montag feels in his memory "the slow simmer" of words from the Bible. At first he remembers the initial verses from Chapter 3 of Ecclesiastes: "To everything there is a season. Yes. A time to break down, and a time to build up. Yes. A time to keep silence and a time to speak. Yes, all that." But The Preacher's words on the vanity of worldly things are not enough for Montag. He tries to remember something else. He digs into his memory for the passage from Revelations 22:2: "*And on either side of the river was there a tree of life, which bare twelve manner of fruits, and yielded her fruit every month; And the leaves of the tree were for the healing of the nations.*" This is the thought Montag wants to reserve for noon, the high point of the day, when they reach the city. Bradbury draws on the Biblical notion of a heavenly Jerusalem, the holy city where men will dwell with God after the apocalypse. Its appeal for Montag is the final stroke of Bradbury's symbolism. In the Bible the heavenly city needs no sun or moon to shine on it, for God's glory is what keeps it lit. The nations of the Earth will walk together by this light, and there will be no night there. The light Montag bears in Granger's remnant of humanity is the Biblical hope for peace and immutability for mankind. This light is the permanent flame Montag has discovered in answer to the devouring nuclear burning invited by Beatty's society and as a counterpoint to the restless Heraclitean fire of the visible cosmos.

From its opening portrait of Montag as a singed salamander, to its concluding allusion to the Bible's promise of undying light for man, *Fahrenheit 451* uses a rich body of symbols emanating from fire to shed a variety of illuminations on future and contemporary man.

To be sure, the novel has its vulnerable spots. For one thing, Montag's opposition is not very formidable. Beatty is an articulate spokesman for the authorities, but he has little of the power to invoke terror that Orwell's

O'Brien has. The Mechanical Hound is a striking and sinister gadget; but for all its silent stalking, it conveys considerably less real alarm than a pack of aroused bloodhounds. What is genuinely frightening is the specter of that witless mass of humanity in the background who feed on manhunts televised live and a gamey version of highway hit-and-run. For another thing, the reader may be unsettled by the vagueness with which Bradbury defines the conditions leading to the nuclear war. Admittedly, his point is that such a lemming-like society, by its very irresponsibility, will ultimately end in destruction. But the reader is justifiably irritated by the absence of any account of the country's political situation or of the international power structure. The firemen are merely enforcers of noninvolvement, not national policy-makers. The reader would like to know something more about the actual controllers of Beatty's occupation. Who, we wonder, is guarding the guardians?

Probably a greater problem than either of these is what some readers may view as a certain evasiveness on Bradbury's part. Presumably, the controversies and conflicts brought on by reading books have led to the system of mass ignorance promulgated by Beatty. Even with this system, though, man drifts into nuclear ruin. Bradbury glosses over the grim question raised by other dystopian novelists of his age: if man's individuality and knowledge bring him repeatedly to catastrophe, should not the one be circumscribed and the other forbidden? Such novels as *A Canticle for Leibowitz*, *A Clockwork Orange*, and *Facial Justice* deal more realistically with this problem than does *Fahrenheit 451*. Although the religious light shining through Montag from the Bible is a fitting climax to the book's use of symbolism, Bradbury's novel does risk lapsing at the very close into a vague optimism.

Yet *Fahrenheit 451* remains a notable achievement in postwar dystopian fiction. Surely it deserves more than its recent dismissal by a noted science fiction critic as "an incoherent polemic against book-burning." The book's weaknesses derive in part from that very symbolism in which its strength and originality are to be found. If *Fahrenheit 451* is vague in political detail, it is accordingly less topical and therefore more broadly applicable to the dilemmas of the twentieth century as a whole. Like the nineteenth-century French symbolists, Bradbury's purpose is to evoke a mood, not to name particulars. His connotative language is far more subtle, his novel far more of one piece, than Huxley's rambling nightmare, *Ape and Essence*. Though the novel lacks the great impact of *Nineteen Eighty-Four*, Kingsley Amis is right when he says that *Fahrenheit 451* is "superior in conciseness and objectivity" to Orwell's anti-utopian novel. If *Fahrenheit 451* poses no genuinely satisfying answers to the plight of postindustrial man, neither is the flight to the stars at the end of *A Canticle for Leibowitz* much of a solution. We can hardly escape from ourselves. By comparison with Bradbury's novel, *Facial Justice* is tepid and *A Clockwork Orange* overdone. On the whole, *Fahrenheit 451* comes out as a distinctive contribution to the speculative literature of our times, because in its multiple variations on its fundamental symbol, it demonstrates that dystopian fiction need not exclude the subtlety of poetry.

WILLIAM F. TOUPONCE

Reverie and the Marvelous: Doublings of the Self in The Martian Chronicles and Fahrenheit 451

In this ⟨essay⟩ we will examine two of Bradbury's early attempts at fantasy in the marvelous and Gothic traditions. I am not so much interested in linking them to these traditions as examples of it as I am in showing how reverie is present as a softening and transforming influence. The first story contains an object reverie and the second an exploration of the splittings and doublings that accompany the *anima-animus dialectic* of reverie. A typical object reverie involves a fathoming of the object in its material intimacy which then offers us a world. Most of us have had the experience of the revelation of a marvelous interior by certain objects: one discovers flowers and figures in the intimacy of frost or crystal, a play of sculpture and design in stone. The object reverie typically goes in a multiple trajectory from exterior to interior, from interior to exterior. Among the objects which privilege this sort of dynamic dreaming consciousness are of course sea shells, and our first story is about the discovery of a fantastic world through inhabiting one. The doublings of the self in reverie are characteristically less harsh and demonic than those of the Gothic, reverie itself being dominated by images of feminine repose. Our second story involves a fantastic world imagined by a woman frustrated by and afraid of her lover in the real world, though she is nonetheless a prodigious dreamer of mutual idealization.

It is no accident that both stories take place on occasions ideal for

From *Ray Bradbury and the Poetics of Reverie.* © 1984 UMI Research Press.

reverie and reading itself in the real world—vacations, periods of recuperation from illness, and lazy, rainy afternoons. In these early stories Bradbury is exploring his strategy for reverie which will later culminate in *The Martian Chronicles* and *Fahrenheit 451* where a whole kaleidoscopic array of reveries is presented to the reader. These novels are in themselves largely self-contained fantasy worlds, not marked by transitions from the ordinary to the fantastic (though it could be argued that *Fahrenheit 451* moves from a fantastic world to a real one). In any case the modern fantastic, as written by Bradbury, does not merely involve the laying bare of Gothic props and supernatural conventions. As always with Bradbury's poetics of reverie, it is a question of having the reader respond to a world and it is this which must be studied.

"The Sea Shell" (1944) was first published in the pulp magazine *Weird Tales,* of interest now because it introduced us to so many American authors of weird and horror fiction: H. P. Lovecraft, Robert Bloch, Clark Ashton Smith, and Bradbury himself, to name just a few. It is one of Bradbury's earliest stories exploring childhood and reverie, creating both suspense and surprise as part of its overall discovery-structure. Because of the typical trajectory of this discovery-structure, "The Sea Shell" is practically an allegory of the reader's task in texts based on reverie and consequently we will want to examine it in some detail. It also contains one of the essential themes of the self in nineteenth-century fantastic literature according to Tzvetan Todorov: metamorphosis or rebirth to another self.

Readers aware of the Romantic tradition will perhaps already have in mind from the title Wordsworth's poetic dream in the fifth book of *The Prelude.* As W. H. Auden points out in his archetypal poetic mediation on this dream of Wordsworth, *The Enchafèd Flood,* the siren voice of the poetic shell calls men to the sea, the double kingdom, to put off their human nature and be trolls. This prospect is alluring to the child in our story (and a rebirth motif is very much in evidence, though subtly handled), but he is not faced with the adult dilemma of the romantic hero according to Auden, which is the danger of becoming through this transformation a purely self-conscious ego. His problem is really the essential problem of adolescence, "that fever of time in human life," as Bachelard says. Initially, his impatience appears to be due to an inability to sublimate in the Freudian manner, deferring his immediate desires with the substitution of another, more socially acceptable object. But actually the sublimation involved is that of reverie for the object does not give rise only to intellectual constructs. It gives rise to a fantastic world. We may call this problem the Omar Khayyam complex, since it is brought out consciously by the boy's mother and therefore the adult perspective, as such. She manifests a wistful kind of sadness towards him, no doubt because she knows what the adult world will do to her boy's dreams. In terms of oneiric criticism, she becomes a kind of anima figure (a feminine character who transmits the reverie object, or helps the reader/dreamer discover his own capacity for reverie, and guides him in that process) as she transmits the reverie object to her son, which provides the means for his escape.

"The Sea Shell" is an allegory of reverie and the reading process because the child's fidelity to the sea shell (often a symbol of psychic transformation and therefore familiar ground in the repertoire) and his persistent day-dreaming of it during his convalescence, allows him to transcend the boredom of his harassed confinement in an act of pure transcendence and flight from the real world. As it turns out, the reader himself has to imagine through a surprise ending how this transcendence came about, but it is nevertheless subliminally prepared for him in descriptions of the child's inner world given by the narrator. In terms of oneiric criticism, this surprise has a later integrative phase, that of Bachelardian reverberation, in which the surprising aspects are seen in connection with what has gone before, with the whole drift of reading experience. In short the reader is brought to a confrontation with his own constitutive activity.

In this manner a dynamic dialectic of inside and out, of familiar and unfamiliar, is generated by the spirals of the reverie object. Primarily we see things from the child's limited point of view. That the child may be carried *too* far away is certainly suggested, since the alluring voices that come from the shell seem to anticipate his reactions. Some readers may feel uneasy about the prospect of the child being trapped in a world so different from that of an adult, but this reaction stems from our sharing of the mother's point of view. Bradbury's basic strategy is to present through a fantastic event the inadequacy of our adult view of things. This in turn releases the reader's spontaneity to seek a deeper understanding of the relationship between childhood imagination and reality.

The plot which underlies this transformation is realistic and straightforward, concerned with the everyday activities of parents and children in the midst of warm domesticity. We are surrounded by what is obviously an American small-town landscape. Johnny Bishop is an eleven-year-old who is simply too impatient to wait a week for his cold to take its natural course. He wants to be out of bed, and outside to play pirate with his friends. The action of the Omar Khayyam complex organizes for the reader all those images and suggestions of compulsive hurrying that appear in the time-flow of reading. The norms of the adult world, the world of constraints on desire and deferral of satisfaction, are represented in the text by the mother. She gives her son a sea shell "to have fun with," hoping that it will ease his impatience. But this only leads to more questions on the part of the boy. The mother finds that she cannot frame an answer to his naive questions about the value of these deferrals. In this manner two very different perspectives are set in a hermeneutic tension and revolve around the sea shell. In the solitude and repose during the next day and night, Johnny begins to inhabit the world of the shell, by listening to the sounds of the imaginary ocean contained in it. This landscape comes more and more to dominate the real world, until supernatural voices beckon the boy to come away. Finally the mother discovers that Johnny is not in his room, and, thinking that he has disobeyed her in running off to play with his friends, she picks up the shell. She hears Johnny playing in the surf when she puts it to her ear.

Having discussed the repertoire and strategies of this text, we can now proceed to treat it as an allegory of our theory of reading. It should be stressed for the sake of clarity however that in general and in all cases where we are dealing with imagistic acts of consciousness produced from a text, to objectivate does not mean to reify. I am simply thematizing and bringing out for analysis those acts of consciousness which were operative in passive syntheses during reading in order to reveal how the process of consistency-building is built up and destroyed, giving rise to the experience of the imaginary and the reader's released spontaneity. Those acts of consciousness described remain dynamic and functional for other readers. Since the story is short, I will quote extensively from it in order to give the reader the all-important sense of context within which reverie develops. It begins by formulating a desire:

> He wanted to get out and run, bounding over hedges, kicking tin cans down the alley, shouting at all the windows for the gang to come and play. The sun was up and the day was bright, and here he was swaddled with bed clothes, sweating and scowling, and not liking it at all.

As we are made familiar with the world of this story in this opening paragraph, we can already sense the presence of a self (or complex) in a childhood landscape and certain magical acts, emotive images, relating to that landscape. There are, in fact, two opposing landscapes that can be observed on closer inspection. One is imaginary and desired, the other is real and frustrating. Thus a subliminal suspense, a tension of inside and out, is generated at the outset. The landscape of activity the boy desires is outside; to escape to it he transforms the frustrating situation inside by recourse to imaginary acts (which are also emotive intentions) that evoke the presence of objects from that desired landscape: an alley, tin cans to kick, windows to shout at, friends to play with. The objects are given as having value within the horizon of his imaginary play on this sunny, bright day. In the imaginary landscape the boy can move freely, without resistance from the pragmatic world. The real world reveals itself as confining, and the boy is "not liking it at all."

The swaddling clothes, objects which resist his activity, also hint at the rebirth motif and at the fact that for the moment he is a helpless baby, a prospect at which he scowls. Because the situation is difficult and he has no means of escape as yet, the boy has unreflectively invested the world with frustration and is living it as such. The swaddling clothes *are* his sweating confinement. It is the world which appears frustrating. However, by an emotional and magical act negating his situation, the boy has also made imaginatively present to us another landscape. There is a strong subliminal link here with the body as landscape. As we shall see, the boy will act on his own sublimatory "lost" body in reverie in order to escape this frustrating situation (in the real world, the fever effectively separates him from his body, makes him self-conscious of it).

The story continues to present more familiar objects of the inside convalescent world subtly transformed by the child's imagination: perfumes (his mother's, orange juice and medicine) evoke the presence of objects that have passed through the atmosphere and are now absent. This scent-laden atmosphere is expressive of a passive mind saturated with emotion and memory, against which the boy rebels. The day is "up," and a shaft of sunlight strikes *down* at him. The patch-work quilt appears to shout at him, just as he imagines shouting at the windows outside. Objects of this world magically shout back at him:

> The entire lower half of the patch-work quilt was a circus banner of red, green, purple and blue. It practically yelled color into his eyes. Johnny fidgeted.
> "I wanna go out," he complained softly. "Darn it. Darn it."
> A fly buzzed, bumping again and again at the window pane with a dry staccato of its transparent wings.
> Johnny looked at it, understanding how it wanted out, too.

A circus is a world of brightly clashing colors which creates at times the magical illusion of flying apart. A multi-colored banner rippling in the wind and sun is its metonymic emblem. The important thing about this emblem (besides the formal tension of its colors) is, phenomenologically, the implied spatial structure which is operative here. The banner is always placed at the top of a pole or mast, overlooking the circus world. The raised position of the banner literally expresses ex-*alta*tion, or the desire to heighten one's life by raising it above the normal level (sublimation in the Bachelardian sense).

Generally, a banner is a sign of victory or self-assertion, but poor Johnny seems wrapped in a defeat which yells color at his eyes. He finds an equivalent for his situation in a not-so-antiseptic creature that normally belongs to the outside world also. The fly "shouts" against the window with its transparent wings that suggest magical flight. As we are made familiar with these objects (the window, the bed-quilt, etc.) we also take over these subliminal, emotive image-structures which appear transformed subtly again in the following sequences (especially the last, where they serve to ground the familiar world which is then abruptly transformed, and through an object with which we are going to be made very familiar: the sea shell).

The mother brings Johnny the bad news that he will have to remain in bed for another two days, a fact that arouses his consternation. He resents having to drink more "healthful" fluids, even if the taste is disguised with orange juice, but the mother offers no medicine this time, only an unfamiliar object:

> "This time—no medicine."
> "What's that in your hand?"
> "Oh, this?" Mother held out a round, spiralled gleaming object.
> Johnny took it. It was hard and shiny and—pretty. "Doctor Hull dropped by a few minutes ago and left it. He thought you might have fun with it."

It should be pointed out that the mother emerges into this conversation from a freshly polished hall shining from the care with which she has touched it. The house is her reverie object, and although she is an adult, as anima figure she still has the sensuous feel for objects that awakens reverie. There is a subliminal suggestion that the boy is already living within a polished shell. Be that as it may, we now find emerging here a network of intentionality surrounding the shell. The doctor sends it as an object intended to be healthful and to assuage the boy's impatience. For her part, the mother transmits these values and shows the boy how to imagine the shell in the next sequence. Because she is an adult, however, she does not transform the shell into a world, although she certainly invests it with value (perhaps she thinks of it as a distraction for her son). Her affective grasp of this object is therefore weak or delicate when compared to the boy's surprise.

The irony is, of course, that the boy will do more than just "have fun" with the shell in rejecting the norms of the adult world. The child will become so familiar with the gift that he genuinely surprises his mother (and us) at the end. He will transform his "Omar Khayyam complex" by living it completely, by transcending it towards a childhood world without parental complexes. For the moment, however, let us note that the shell forms the center of a developing narrative network embracing all the characters. Johnny's first perception of the inanimate shell is from the outside; it is seen as having a humanly-defined lure of prettiness whose resistant textures (hard and shiny and spiralled) invite a loving caress. But the boy is dubious, perhaps because the object *is* unfamiliar, and he needs to classify it before he will accept it:

> Johnny looked palely dubious. His small hands brushed the slick surface. "How can I have fun with it? I don't even know what it is!"
>
> Mother's smile was better than sunshine. "It's a shell from the sea, Johnny. Doctor Hull picked it up on the Pacific shore last year when he was out there."
>
> "Hey, that's all right. What kind of shell is it?"
>
> "Oh, I don't know. Some form of sea life probably lived in it once, a long time ago."
>
> Johnny's brows went up. "Lived in this? Made it a home?"
>
> "Yes."
>
> "Aw—really?"
>
> She adjusted it in his hand. "If you don't believe me, listen for yourself, young man. Put this end—here—against your ear."
>
> "Like this?" He raised the shell to his small pink ear and pressed it tight. "Now what do I do?"
>
> Mother smiled. "Now, if you're very quiet, and listen closely, you'll hear something very, very familiar."
>
> Johnny listened. His ear opened imperceptibly like a small flower opening, waiting.
>
> A titanic wave came in on a rocky shore and smashed itself down.
>
> "The sea!" cried Johnny Bishop. "Oh, Mom! The ocean! The waves! The sea!"
>
> Wave after wave came in on that distant, craggy shore. Johnny closed his eyes tight black and a smile folded his face exactly in half. Wave after pounding wave roared in his small pinkly alert ear.
>
> "Yes, Johnny," said Mother. "The sea."

Another landscape (still distant because the child is not immersed in it as yet) has been made imaginatively present. The mother's magic (the magic of the Other in transforming *my* world) is to transform Johnny's world from the outside. She shows him the very familiar in the unfamiliar, teaching him to discover the marvelous by patient listening to the reverberation of images (Bachelard's *retentissement*). The sea shell is indeed a marvelous reverie object because it contains within it an intimate immensity—the boy can hold the ocean in the palm of his hand. At the beginning of this passage the shell is somewhat of an empty schema for the child. He has no knowledge of it other than what is given in perception or from his mother who guides him through this reverie experience. He is given some knowledge of it from her (she tells him it is from the Pacific shore) which he then fills in with affective intentions in order to transform his situation. The shell is first hypothesized as containing life (the waves have the activity and weight of bodies here)— which the child initially disputes. The boy is dubious about any living creature wanting to live in such a confined space. But then he is asked to listen (imagine for himself) in order to discover that life. He discovers to his surprise the internal landscape of the sea within it. Magically, the sea shell works a kind of spell on him. Coming from the Other, and yet being safe, it shatters the pragmatic order of the day by disrupting his expectations.

But Johnny also acts unreflectively on himself. He "lives" this illusion in which the world seems changed. He is able to inhabit this magical world in an instant, through the phenomenon of belief created by the incantation of the waves pounding on the beach. Now, these imaginative acts are already a transformation of the world which has become too difficult for him. They are the means by which he apprehends this new and unfamiliar object. Imagination in reverie is therefore not merely the filling in of empty schemas of knowledge with images. It is also the magical emotive transformation of those objects as we would like them to be (and just for the sake of oneiric verisimilitude, Bradbury has us learn in the next section that the boy has never *seen* the ocean but is working from analogies of a local lake by exaggerating images. Exaggeration, according to Bachelard, is the surest sign of wonder).

Normally, we learn about new objects through perception, that is, by *degrees*. They offer solid resistance to our attempts to know them; they are never (or rarely) seen as totalities, only as given in perspective, in facets. In fact the boy expresses his *impatience* with this perceptual process. How can I have fun with it, he says, if I don't know what it is, as if only those things which offer instantaneously the promise of a world (namely, images) are worthy enough to hold a world of freedom. The mother hopes to teach the boy patience by listening, but we can see that he has discovered that reverie negates a problematic world of frustration and setbacks (the adult world) by offering an instantaneous transformation in which we "live" our desires. And it must be persistently believed in, dreamt with fidelity, if it is to rival the real world. As we shall see, that is exactly what Johnny does in the following sequences.

But what of the reader's role thus far? Has his capacity for reverie been activated? Bachelard himself was extremely fond of shells, but he points out in *The Poetics of Space*, where he devotes an entire chapter to them, that the material imagination suffers a kind of defeat before this beautifully formal object. For Bachelard the shell would seem a triumph of the formal imagination, nature herself having dreamt pure geometry in a spiral that nevertheless represents the life force itself. How is it possible, Bachelard wonders, to surpass nature in her own dream? Perhaps, Bachelard suggests, we should begin phenomenologically with the naive observer, the child, before the object which will invite his daydream. Now, because the shell is a hollow object that once contained life, it has borne the traditional associations of the allegory of body and soul. In order to avoid these scholarly accretions therefore what one needs to consider is the "function of inhabiting" these objects. This will counter the classifying tendencies of the conchologist.

Then, says Bachelard, a lively dialectics of childhood wonderment emerges. In the textual play of his own meditation Bachelard considers many descriptions of melusines and fantastic monsters that dreamers have imagined to inhabit empty shells. He comments on fantastic texts where wondrously large creatures, like elephants, emerge from small shells, activating a dialectics of large and small. The phenomenologist's imagination is also stimulated by the dialectics of creatures that are free and others that are in fetters. Bachelard notes however that this exercise often leads to a fear-curiosity complex. We want to see what is in the shell, but we are afraid of what might leap out at us:

> These undulations of fear and curiosity increase when reality is not there to moderate them, that is, when we are imagining. However, let's not invent, but rather give documents concerning images which have actually been imagined or drawn, and which have remained engraved in precious and other stones. There is a passage in the book by Jurgis Baltrusaitis in which he recalls the *action* of an artist who shows a dog that "leaps from its shell" and pounces upon a rabbit. One degree more of aggressiveness and the shell-dog would attack a man. This is a clear example of the progressing type of action by means of which imagination surpasses reality. For here the imagination acts upon not only geometrical dimensions, but upon elements of power and speed as well—not in an enlarged space, either, but in a more rapid tempo. When the motion picture camera accelerates the unfolding of a flower, we receive a sublime image of offering; it

is as though the flower we see opening so quickly and without reservation, sensed the meaning of a gift; as though it were a gift from the world. But if the cinema showed us a snail emerging from its shell in fast motion, or pushing its horns toward the sky very rapidly, what an aggression that would be! What aggressive horns! All our curiosity would be blocked by fear, and the fear-curiosity complex would be torn apart.

It should now be apparent that we have not been wandering from our topic, the reader's role, as might first have seemed. The undulating spiral of fear and curiosity is not allowed to increase (as yet) because reality *is* there in our story in the form of a generalized schema of a shell to moderate it. The mother is guiding the reader as well, by assuring him that Johnny is going to find something very very familiar in the shell. We are assured that no fantastic animal is going to suddenly leap upon us—as perhaps would happen in some weird or horror stories. Our imagination is not allowed aggressively to surpass reality.

Furthermore, the fear aspect of this reading complex is softened by the narrator's flower image, which offers to the reader the promise of a safe refuge in inhabiting the shell. We can describe phenomenologically how this feeling is established for the reader by passive syntheses in the following manner. The reader has first of all to build up a series of equivalences between flower and shell. A flower is a formal image, equivalent to a shell in that respect, but unlike a shell it is rapidly opening, suggesting a certain dynamism. An open image is the only image sure to bring about reverie. Second, Johnny's ear opens imperceptibly. We are not asked to perceive, but to imagine a small flower opening, waiting. The flower image is not just a static metaphor, but suggests an equivalent to Johnny's experience which is in the nature of a guarded, protected opening to an as yet strange and unfamiliar world. The reader's further imagination of Johnny's ear as another kind of shell, small and pink, is thus mediated by an oneiric image, hence its central position in this passage.

Thus the oneiric level of the text aids us imperceptibly in integrating two dimensions of experience, self and world. The flower image presents the reader with interiority that invites intimacy; it gives him the assurance that he is going to link up oneiric relations that reverie will make inexhaustible in this new world. In short, the flower defines the reader's imaginative position in an instantaneous act of consciousness: the reader is centered as in the center of a flower, surrounded by rays of color in the delicately nuanced petals of meaning. And if we now consider Bachelard's fantasy about the rapidly opening flower, then this surprise image of offering can be linked back oneirically to the doctor's and the mother's gifts. This surprise linking introduces an oneiric level of significance to narrative consciousness, tells us that the reverie world offers itself as a flower to us, and assures us that we will inhabit this world without fear.

At the end of this sequence, when the waves wash refreshingly again and again over it, Johnny's ear is practically a small pink creature inhabiting the shell. If he is then a creature "in fetters" in the large shell of the house, then one definitely gets the feeling that he is going to prepare this small space as a means of dynamic escape. His ear is now "pinkly alert," that is, now that the equivalence of the house and shell have been established by an oneiric logic of invention (if the entire sea can be contained in such a small space, why not a boy?). Johnny closes his eyes "tight black," smiling broadly, no longer wanting to consider the shell in formal imagination. No longer respecting form or color (those stable things) he is seized by a conviction of a refuge in which life can be concentrated and then transcended by leaping to meet the in-coming waves.

Let us now summarize the passive syntheses that we have made thematic in the past few pages. Initially, the boy is seduced by the unfamiliar formal and sensuous beauty of the shell. He wants to classify it in order to play with it in an exterior fashion. This is as far as Freudian sublimation would go—the limit of the concept. The shell is then hypothesized as containing life, but the boy is dubious about any creature wanting to inhabit such a small space. It seems a very small and confining world indeed. The mother/anima figure then guides the boy by putting the shell to his ear so that he can "believe" in the statement she has made. Then, as we have seen, this gesture activates the fantasy of rebirth to another world. Johnny finally leaves behind the formal imagination (which, as Bachelard says, defeats the production of images) and establishes an imaginative grounding in *matter*, the water which will underlie and sustain the play of surface imagery in the third sequence. Johnny can hear the play of his friends outside:

> Their voices seemed so far away, lazy, drifting on a tide of sun. The sunlight was just like deep yellow, lambent water, lapping at the summer, full tide. Slow, languorous, warm, lazy. The whole world was over its head in that tide and everything was slowed down. The clock ticked slower. The street car came down the avenue in warm metal slow motion. It was almost like seeing a motion film that is losing speed and noise. Everything was softer. Nothing seemed to count as much.
>
> He wanted to get out and play, badly. He kept watching the kids climbing the fences, playing soft ball, roller skating in the

warm languor. His head felt heavy, heavy, heavy. His eyelids were window sashes pulling down, down. The sea shell lay against his ear. He pressed it close.

Pounding, drumming, waves broke on a shore. A yellow sand shore. And when the waves went back out they left foam, like the suds of beer, on the sand. The suds broke and vanished, like dreams. And more waves came with more foam. And the sand crabs tumbled, salt-wet, scuttling brown, in the ripples. Cool green water pounding on the sand. The very sound of it conjured up visions; the ocean breeze soothed Johnny Bishop's small body. Suddenly the hot afternoon was no longer hot and depressing. The clock started ticking faster. The street cars clanged metal quickly. The slowness of the summer world was spanked into crisp life by the pound-pound of waves on an unseen and brilliant beach.

Insofar as I have been able to determine, this is the earliest example in Bradbury's fantasy of a deliberately narrated daydream. As such, it is an exemplary illustration of a dreaming subject going into image-making reverie in an imaginary landscape unseen yet brilliant. It unfolds in three phases which are coherent deformations of each other. The dozing style of the first phase seems to me to evoke the mingling of memory and imagination. It suggests long solitary hours spent lying idle on the beach at Fox Lake, where we know the boy has vacationed before. It is the recollection of a real landscape of gently lapping water that gradually immerses the real world with the help of the boy's imagination. Once he finds his element he wants to develop it further, to sublimate it further from small lake to ocean. As the boy half shuts his eyes in the lazy warmth, the two landscapes, real and imagined, seem to melt into each other. The world seems bathed in the languorous yellow light of this remembered daydream; indeed, it appears to be underwater (suggesting the pastness of the past), and objects of the familiar outside world are being slowed down by the resistance of the tide of liquid sun. Notice especially the "far away" perception of objects that are softened by reverie into meaning less than they normally do as utensils in the real world. The metal of the street car is on the verge of a surreal deformation.

The same phenomenological psychology that was operative before is again operative here—he finds the world difficult and tries to escape, this time by falling back into a reverie he had experienced long ago, one which has been reactivated by his discovery of the sea shell's reverberating interiority. It is thus the reverie object which activates the archetype of watery rebirth, but I am not arguing for any causal determinism here. The real world in fact appears to be losing speed and time—and its grip on him. No doubt the boy has something of a fever, but convalescence here is simply a metaphor for reverie (in one of his aphorisms Bachelard asks us: is not every convalescence a childhood?). The body is again the substratum for reverie. The text gives us a humorous comparison of the boy's eyes closing like window sashes shutting out the unreachable desired world of play outside. It is a familiar enough metaphor, but appropriate to the hypnagogic phases of reverie where acts of consciousness may take on a dramatized form. Of course the whole point of the metaphor is to show us that the boy does not *want* to fall asleep where he would be something less than an active subject pursuing his own intentions.

The only recourse is to evoke a world of activity, and when the boy puts the shell to his ear in the second phase, we enter reverie proper. The beach is described as an independent world, as brilliant yet unseen. No transition is given by the narrator; the world is magically *there*, rivalling the real world through the incantation of its waves. The shell recalls the yellow sand shore of its origin, and takes the boy with it. The water of the sea is, however, unlike that of the lake. It is a force which produces new images, thousands of them. The archetypal foam is full of bubble-dreams, visions of worlds possible if evanescent.

All of this shows us that once the imagination touches matter in reverie, it produces multivalent, excessive beauty, and psychic well-being. Notice, for example, the healthful activity of the little sand crabs who are so obviously seen as aggressively tanned by the sun. Reverie has dislodged and jostled the very adjectives that describe their behavior out of their familiar positions: they are imagined as dynamic and moving, tumbled, salt-wet, scuttling brown. If given free rein, reverie often plays with words in this fashion, creating surprise by new syntactic relationships among words, but there are never any violent eruptions of nonsense which are irreducible to meaning. In the unconscious field we may experience a complete lapsus of the word; in reverie the archetypal element, the substance being imagined, controls the play of linguistic signs. In this world the cold splash of the waves provides a material resistance and meaning stimulating to the imagination, a kind of joyful intentionality that experiences a force in directing itself towards an object. It is altogether different from the sweating adversity of the boy's bed clothes.

In the third and final phase, Johnny returns to the real world which is seen as refreshed, and moving faster from his reverie activity. The ocean breeze has soothed his body—again, an indication of how the unreflective emotive intentions of reverie act magically to transform the world by influencing the body. The summer world is spanked into crisp life, a metaphor of rebirth, of course, but perhaps also recalling the image of the doctor who picked up the shell. There is not as yet a completely independent fantastic world however. It is only the real world which has been rejuvenated. But by virtue of this experience of imaginary meaning sustained by acts of consciousness based on archetypal matter, by the fact that its beautiful and new images are born in the dreamer's solitude away from the real world of perception, by virtue of the fact that the dreamer ventures far away to recover these riches, and by virtue of the well-being it creates, we can call this passage a successful reverie. That the child is a persistent day-dreamer is indicated in the narrator's summary that follows this passage, a passage which estimates the value of the shell in days to come. It is a means to keep temporality flowing onwards toward the future.

There is one aspect of reverie which we first mentioned in our brief summary in the introduction that as yet we have not discussed, namely, its cosmic power of origination. This is actually the most important dimension of reverie, but I have put off discussion of it until the fourth narrative sequence because it is made thematic for the reader there. The fourth sequence is a cognitive attempt at a "philosophy of childhood." The reader is asked to consider the child's desire and imagination in a much larger context which reflects the possibilities of man as a conscious being. There is an allusion from the repertoire to the *Rubaiyat* of Omar Khayyam (whose verse form, the *ruba'i*, was said to have been accidentally discovered by a poet who overheard the gleeful shout of a child at play and adopted it) to aid the reader in understanding the problem of the conflict or problematic opposition of the world of childhood and the adult's world. The dialogue takes the form of a lesson about the necessity, from the adult's point of view, of acquiring the attributes of maturity: waiting, planning, and above all being patient (there is probably a pun on being a patient and impatience). Yet there is no doubt where the sympathy of the reader should lie, because the mother herself feels the loss of her own childhood in the eyes of her son, which are wide and full of the blue light of his imaginary ocean. Her lesson is therefore somewhat reversed on her.

Now, the boy has learned through the persistence of his daydream the power of cosmic origination in reverie. With that power the boy can say "no" to the adult world even as the new world of reverie opens up for him (symbolically expressed by the shell which he keeps listening to and putting against his ear throughout the lesson). He is no longer completely captive in the world of adults, and we have seen him play with this new-found power (which some parental readers may find anxiety-provoking) in the narrated daydream of the third sequence. Iser might say that what the child has learned, though he cannot at this stage explicitly formulate it, is that his acts are not determined. Imaginative acts of consciousness are caused by nothing but consciousness itself; indeed, they are the characteristic free functioning of childhood consciousness (as readers, we share these acts of imaginative consciousness and spontaneously give our own as well, so it can be said that they are characteristic of adult consciousness as well—a point which I will elaborate in my summary of the reader's discovery in this text). Johnny is a free, if perhaps not entirely responsible, agent. His great discovery is that there is a world of oneiric possibility superadded to the world of reality. The boy is not restricted to the real, for he can enter at will the realm of the ideal through the reverie object. He has the power to negate the actual and actualize the merely possible. Why should he not be intoxicated with this magic power (the sea foam is compared to suds of beer, we remember) and be very reluctant to give it up. Most importantly, however, the child's accession to the freedom of reverie is a break with reality, a rupture which refuses the adult world in creating its own. Johnny's questioning and contrary attitude in this sequence is an important indication that he finds the adult world inadequate and incomplete. The child's imagination is not, therefore, perception revivified, but a characteristic function of human consciousness which transforms the world by the power of negation.

As the end of the third sequence, Johnny had asked his mother about going to the seashore as soon as possible (he imagines the sea as being better than Fox Lake) not being willing to wait for his father's two-week vacation in July. Now the mother tries to teach him patience:

> Mother sat down on the bed and held his hand. The things she said he couldn't understand fully, but some of them made sense. "If I had to write a philosophy of children, I guess I'd title it impatience. Impatience with everything in life . . . You're a tribe of potential Omar Khayyams, that's what."

She reminds him of the attributes of maturity and he responds:

> "I don't wanna be patient. I don't like being in bed. I want to go to the sea shore."

The mother tries to mediate the problem of childhood by offering an example from her own childhood:

> "I remember, I saw a doll once when I was a girl. I told my mother about it, said it was the last one for sale, I said I was afraid it would be sold before I could get it. The truth of the matter is

there were a dozen others just like it. I couldn't wait. I was impatient, too."

Johnny shifted on the bed. His eyes widened and got full of blue light. "But Mom, I don't want to wait. If I wait too long, I'll be grown up, and then it won't be any fun."

Obviously, the mother does not want the boy to lie about how well he feels, but the boy's remark about the adult world stifling the fun of things (it doesn't matter how *many* dolls, or sea shells, there are in truth, he seems to say, what matters is having one as a reverie object for one's childhood—otherwise, what would one have to look back on from adulthood if one was never allowed to develop reveries during this precious time) brings the mother to the brink of tears:

> ". . . Sometimes I think you're—right. But I don't dare tell you. It isn't according to the rules—"
>
> "What rules, Mom?"
>
> "Civilization's. Enjoy yourself, while you are young. Enjoy yourself, Johnny." She said it strong, and funny-like.
>
> Johnny put the shell to his ear. "Mom. Know what I'd like to do? I'd like to be at the seashore right now, running towards the water, holding my nose and yelling 'Last one in is a double-darned monkey!'" Johnny laughed.
>
> The phone rang downstairs. Mother walked to answer it.
>
> Johnny lay there, quietly, listening.

Teaching the reader an unexpected lesson about the necessity of childhood reverie, the mother's attempt to mediate the values of civilization and its discontents (the renunciation of reverie, if not of instinct) to the child has backfired. The equivalences she offers as a bridge of understanding all fail before the boy's desire. She must listen to the pragmatic voices of the adult world, symbolized by the telephone, while her son listens to the call of the sea. Putting the shell to his ear, the child again makes a gesture of commitment to his reverie world. This kind of reversal of intention will be repeated at the end of the last sequence when the mother puts the shell to her ear and hears supernatural voices; in fact she hears the exact same words: "Last one in is a double-darned monkey." This doubling or echoing shatters the framework of everyday reality as her own son becomes a supernatural Other transforming her world from the "outside," that is, from the world within the shell. Thus the reader is made familiar here with a challenging phrase that will return to surprise and perhaps mock him in a fantastic mode. It could be argued that this repetition brings about an uncanny effect of meaning in the reader, but it is actually more in the nature of a fulfillment of meaning postulated as an empty intention earlier.

Certainly is intensifies the problem of a "philosophy of childhood" of whose meaning we might have thought ourselves master. We learn that the language and attitude towards the problem of childhood expressed by the mother, while pretending to be univocal, actually admits to having a double meaning. Children are a potential tribe of Omar Khayyams, always wanting to shatter the schema of things and refashion it closer to the heart's desire (the XCIX stanza of the *Rubaiyat*). Thus the phrase "to have fun with," repeated several times in the story, comes to mean quite different things to the mother than to the boy. The mother thinks that the schema of things, the harsh rule of the reality principle and civilization, cannot be broken, but in the story's marvelous ending, they are. This surprise causes the reader to reexamine the nature of the relationship between imagination and reality, to reconsider a philosophy which represses what childhood reverie does with language, and to formulate for himself the ways in which that schema, which seems so solid, can be broken together with the value of breaking it.

The mother/anima figure raises the possibility that a philosophy of childhood could be written. Bachelard's texts affirm that it can, although in ways subtly subversive of philosophic conceptual mastery itself. We ourselves have been reading (or rather writing about) this story as if it were an allegory of childhood and reverie, as if the entire text had the effect of being an illustration of that idea. As Todorov points out, this procedure is a meta-reading which to an extent falsifies the all-important temporal and experiential structure of fantasy texts. Knowing the end destroys the function of hesitation on which the genre seems to depend. For Todorov, the fantastic is a genre of "emphatic temporality." It is essential in his view that a reading of the fantastic follow that of the reader in his identification with a character step by irreversible step. We too want to follow the flow of reading and not to impose artificial constructs, yet this procedure is justified here because the reader's double role in "The Sea Shell" directs him to reconsider retrospectively and reflectively the relationship of imagination to reality he held prior to reading. In philosophical terms, when the empty schema of the shell is marvelously "filled in" with supernatural voices at the end, we wonder how the boy manages to be absent from the world yet present in language at the same time. Our allegorical reading does not therefore destroy the effect of the fantastic, so much as it does thematize how that effect is brought about through the experience of the imaginary, the ontological significance of which the reader has to search for at the end. Let us therefore consider how the themes and elements of the fantastic emerge in the fifth sequence.

There is first of all the reader's hesitation (constituting what in Todorov's view is the evanescent theoretical genre of the pure fantastic) about the supernatural voices that emerge from the shell. Is the boy imagining them or are they real? The narrator gives us no indication but records the character's own surprise and hesitation on hearing them. We are still very much in the adult scheme of things at the beginning of this sequence. However, a dynamic tension between two landscapes is again conveyed through an oneiric window-metaphor: stars are caught in the squared glass corrals of the big window. This suggested equivalence beings about a child's view of the night sky's constellations as brightly moving animal figures that have been imprisoned, and lends a sense of cosmic sympathy to the boy's situation. But from this confining boundary or frame to the end of the story, the events move away from the world of everyday reality to end in what Todorov would classify as a fantastic-marvelous situation, defined as a hesitation between the real and the imaginary where the supernatural has not yet been accepted. Following the character's emotive intentions, the reader has thus far assumed that Johnny was imagining that shore inside the shell, but now autonomous voices appear:

> Johnny closed his eyes. Downstairs, silverware was being clattered at the dinner table. Mom and Pop were eating. He heard Pop laughing his deep laughter.
>
> The waves still came in, over and over, on the shore inside the sea shell. And—something else.
>
> "Down where the waves lift, down where the waves play, down where the gulls swoop low on a summer's day—"
>
> "Huh?" Johnny listened. His body stiffened. He blinked his eyes.
>
> Softly, way off:
>
> "Stark ocean sky, sunlight on waves. Yo ho, heave ho, heave ho, my braves—"
>
> It sounded like a hundred voices singing to the creak of oarlocks.
>
> "Come down to the sea in ships—"
>
> And then another voice, all by itself, soft against the sound of waves and ocean wind.
>
> "Come down to the sea, the contortionist sea, where the great tides wrestle and swell. Come down to the salt in the glittering brine, on a trail that you'll soon know well—"
>
> Johnny pulled the shell from his head, stared at it.
>
> "Do you want to come down to the sea, my lad, do you want

to come down to the sea? Well, take me by the hand, my lad, just take me by the hand, my lad, and come along with me!"

Trembling, Johnny clamped the shell to his ear again, sat up in bed, breathing fast. His small heart leaped and hit the wall of his chest.

The presence of these legendary voices is full of the dynamic activity the child desires. They could be pirates or Sinbad the sailor's men, a tribe of potential Omar Khayyams. Interacting with the sea by rowing rhythmically, they chant of magical pathways among the waves. But we do not respond merely to linguistic speech acts. There is again the attraction of shining, gleaming, glittering things from a landscape brilliant but unseen. Bright colors, pungent smells, and seductive words and gestures call for the boy to immerse himself in their collective action. Then a single voice separates itself from this chanting and invites him to come down to the "contortionist" sea "on a path that you'll soon know well." The very idea of the sea as a contortionist suggests the acrobatic transformation of the self into some extraordinary fantastic position. The ordinary and regular paths of the adult world (which the boy has spent so much time emotively negating) are to be magically replaced by a trail the boy will soon know well by some sleight of hand. Clearly, the voice anticipates his inmost desire, surprising and shattering his expectations. The voice comes from the realm of the supernatural Other, but it is nevertheless a guiding voice that tells him he will soon be very familiar with something. It thus quickly establishes its benign nature by mimicking the anima's safe and gradual guidance. It may be demonic, but the surrounding voices are soft, insistent, and Johnny's small heart leaps at the thought of taking part in such rhythmic activity, and by this we know he is already magically transforming his body to meet it. The dialectics of inside and out takes one more step in telling Johnny that the path to the sea-water world lies in the mysterious imagination of the shell's exterior form (the mother had directed his attention to the inside after luring him with exterior prettiness):

"Have you ever seen a fine conch-shell, shaped and shined like a pearl corkscrew? It starts out big and it ends up small, seemingly ending with nothing at all, but, aye lad, it ends where the sea-cliffs fall; where the sea-cliffs fall to the blue!"

These internally rhyming lines contain the pleasure of novelty and surprise (in seeing words dissimilar in meaning appear similar in sound) while creating a kind of enclosing spell. The spiral is a synthesis of both big and small, a path of infinite imagination that only seems to end up with nothing (complete negation and loss of the real) but actually reveals its own world in the frozen image of a wave at play. Johnny recognizes that the shell points in an imaginary direction, out of this world:

> Johnny's fingers tightened on the circular marks of the shell. That was right. It went around and around and around until you couldn't see it going around any more.
>
> Johnny's lips tightened. What was it mother had said? Children. The—the philosophy—what a big word! of children! Impatience. Impatience! Yes, yes, he was impatient! Why not? His free hand clenched into a tiny hard white fist, pounding against the covers.

The last gesture is indeed a magical action! Johnny's hand has become a wave pounding on the beach. He has transformed his mother's philosophy of children into action, by making his hand into the image of a wave. Why not, he thinks, negating the adult world, and the reader may find that he himself has accepted these supernatural events as marvelous, as Johnny seems to here. At any rate, we can understand why he chooses to hide the precious shell from his father when he comes to say goodnight. The world of the child should remain separate from the adult world, we feel. Yet the reader's fear-curiosity complex *is* aroused. In the mother's philosophy, the shell can always be removed from one's ear, one's impatience having been temporarily assuaged, and it is therefore an object belonging to the larger instrumental complex of the adult world. But if the shell is itself a world, then the boy is lost to us. As I have mentioned, some readers may feel a strong sense of menace in the way these voices seem to anticipate his reactions. However, I find the subliminal suggestion of fear so softened by the boy's obvious enjoyment and well-being in the reverie world that I do not fear for him at all. My fear and surprise are rather for the mother in the last sequence.

The sixth and final sequence is told from the mother's point of view, that is, from the point of view of one who possesses the philosophic attributes of maturity, but also an embarrassed sympathy for the child's imagination. At the end of the fifth sequence, we are held in suspense, wondering whether the voices will be seen to be illusory or not. We carry forward our hesitation into this last sequence, which at first seems to modulate towards what Todorov calls the supernatural explained (the uncanny). But the story then spirals down to a surprise ending—a quality which is difficult to capture in quotation. First of all the boy *is* absent from the scene, we do not as yet know where, but all the familiar objects the boy has invested with emotive intentions return. Through a succession of empty objects that are nevertheless subliminally suggested as filled (and this juxtaposition leads the reader, but not the mother, to the oneiric level) we can feel that the boy has escaped:

> The bed was empty. There was nothing but sunlight and silence in the room. Sunlight lay abed, like a bright patient with its brilliant head on the pillow. The quilt, a red-blue circus banner, was thrown back. The bed was wrinkled like the face of a pale old man, and it was very empty.

Daydreaming sunlight, which emanates from the outside world, has taken Johnny's place. The circus banner that confined him is thrown back, abandoned, which reveals the bed itself as transformed to an old man, wrinkled and empty. These images go beyond the obvious rejection-of-adulthood motif—they hint at a transformation of self to a world where youth is forever preserved against the onset of adulthood. They suggest a world transcended. The mother hypothesizes that the child has run outside to play with "those neighbor ruffians." As the mother begins to adjust the quilt into place (trying to rearrange things back to the paths of the ordinary and orderly world) and to smooth the sheets, she discovers that the bed is *not* empty. The shell is there. It appears again as unfamiliar in perception. The mother beings forth "a shining object into the sun." This image hints again at the rebirth motif, for a child is unfamiliar to its mother at birth. She smiles, recognizing it as familiar, and perhaps to remember her own childhood or her son who she assumes is now absent, puts the shell to her ear "just for fun" and receives the shock of her life:

> The room whirled around in a bright swaying merry-go-round of bannered quilts and glassed run.
> The sea shell roared in her ear.

The mother's sudden vertiginous loss of reality, the shattering of the adult scheme of things, is conveyed by the rapid motion of the merry-go-round, an object which itself bears connotations of the return of childhood time. We feel that she is instantaneously thrown into this fantastic world, which the narrator now presents without comment, leaving an ellipsis or indeterminacy for the reader at the end:

> Waves thundered on a distant shore. Waves foamed cool on a far off beach.

So far, these images are very much like those Johnny discovered in his reverie of the shell, and they could be her reverie, but:

> Then the sound of small feet crunching swiftly in the sand.
> A high young voice yelling:
> "Hi! Come on, you guys! Last one in is a double-darned monkey!"
> And the sound of a small body diving, splashing, into those waves . . .

So the story ends, on a fantastic-marvelous event. As Tolkien would perhaps say, the sea shell was no more us than we were it. The reader's spontaneity has been released; the child has become totally Other, transforming the mother's world from the outside (which is also, of course, the inside of a shell). A reverie object of the inside familiar world suddenly reveals its potential to shatter the scheme of things, teaching the mother a lesson in the "philosophy of childhood." The sea shell was an instrument of deferral in the hands of the mother, a world of reverie to the boy, and a means of marvelous escape to whatever supernatural beings seemed to inhabit it. The reader is left with the impossibility of accepting this event as a hallucination—we are given too much of a grounding in the familiar world of the mother to believe that *she* is sick or feverish. Neither can we acquiesce in the pure marvelous, as in a fairy tale, where events of this nature would provoke no surprise. It seems to me that the reader is left with a problem of working out for himself the relationships of imagination and reality that have played back and forth throughout this story.

Summarizing the reader's double role, we can say that the sea shell of our story receives different imaginative values from two perspectives: that of the adult and that of the child. As the story progresses, it functions as a center for intentional acts of consciousness that are instrumental in building up Johnny's sublimative reverie world and in destroying the limited perspectives of the adult world. With the surprise ending the reader is directed towards the oneiric level of the text from which he must build up an adequate "philosophy of childhood." Offering a transcendent vantage point, this level allows the reader to explore existentially his own capacity for reverie. Just as in the experience of the fantastic according to Todorov, the implied reader of "The Sea Shell" is required to judge certain events while identifying himself with a character. Yet these events are so structured by the text that recollecting and anticipatory acts of consciousness on the part of the reader lend it a kind of reflective depth that Bachelard calls reverberation. The reader must build up a system of equivalences between the two perspectives that culminates in the emergence of the aesthetic object, the shell as world. Our surprise at this world "fills in" the passive and provisional syntheses that went before with a more active significance.

Because the shell is only a schema in a story (picking up our allegorical reading again), it solicits us to imagine it, *as* imagined by the characters of the story who represent the norms of the adult and childhood worlds in conflict. The sea shell reverberates with this conflict as it comes to consciousness in the reader's mind. We reexperience their intentions, but the shell itself remains a beautiful formal object. Only its significance changes, due to the affective intentions, strong or weak, of the characters. As long as we remain on the emotive level (which is basically unreflective) we live this story by our own imaginative acts of consciousness. But reverie becomes a magical world *for us*, we double ourselves in the midst of the pragmatic world we have for the moment suspended. The story would not be able to have the effect on us that it does (the search for the meaning of childhood imagination) if we did not constitute it, however unreflectively, for ourselves first. In that regard, we can agree with Todorov. But the last magical transformation of the shell defeats our expectations, surprises us. We are confronted with our own emotive acts of consciousness as magical,—the very ones we used to constitute a fantastic world—and as we see the mother's world transformed into a dizzying merry-go-round by the supernatural Other. We realize that the shell has been made to conform to the child's ideal image of it, that is, as a world of oneiric activity apart from the adult world, containing him—what he wanted it to be all along. The boy's feelings, we realize, have remade the world closer to his heart's desire. How this occurrence came about we are not told, the text remains in the fantastic-marvelous, and we must re-search the problematic relation between the real and the imaginary.

The reader's unreflective imaginary possession of this story and its reverie object, the sea shell, will lead him later to several discoveries about reverie itself, which we are now prepared to summarize. First of all, we can say that "The Sea Shell" has enriched our understanding of the relationship between the imagination of childhood and the largely perceptual (or so Bradbury presents it) world of adults. Perceptual objects, like the shell, yield themselves only by degrees, never all at once, as in the magical image. There is great pleasure in considering objects for their formal beauty, but their real value can be discovered only by inhabiting them. Second, we realize that should the sea shell have appeared unaccompanied by imaginative transformation, we would have experienced a singularly impoverished world. The childhood imagination in reverie seeks to change the merely perceived by making up for what is lacking in the adult world. Lastly, this magical and emotive transformation of things closer to the heart's desire *is* based on what is known in perception, but it is not merely a reproduction of it. In reverie the image-making powers of the mind are a synthesis of the emotive and the cognitive.

Considered as an objective verbal document, "The Sea Shell" is not the equal in style to some of Bradbury's later accomplishments with object reveries in the context of the family, which we will examine in later chapters. It has a tendency to make its theme—a philosophy of childhood—all too sentimentally obvious. Nevertheless, Bradbury does use those phenomenological elements of the reading process we have outlined—recognition and grounding in the familiar repertoire, expectation, imagistic surprise which then leads to discovery—to enable the reader to constitute one of the major themes of all his work, namely, a philosophy of childhood. The reader of "The Sea Shell" discovers a resultant world composed on the basis of the old and familiar adult world, but yet entirely new and unique, transformed by childhood imagination. As in all texts based on reverie, the reader is compelled to imagine an intimate relation with the cosmos and to wonder at the sudden illumination of the image which opens on another fantastic world.

A sophisticated reader might be inclined to smile at such childish enthusiasms. But Bradbury, in having the reader identify with his character, Johnny Bishop, really returns him to the thing itself, the sea shell, as constituted by a purely phenomenological consciousness, which, because of its extreme naiveté, is without preconceptions. We follow the naive consciousness of the boy imagining the sea shell and gather for ourselves images that suggest a sublimatory capacity for renewal. The reader discovers, in short, a rebirth of his own childhood imagination. Inside the small shell time speeds up in marvelous ways, distance is magically abolished, the reader's imagination bathes in the cosmic rhythms of the sea. Bradbury's formal re-imagining of the shell's spiral has generated a story which begins with traditional images and associations but which does not allow the reader to crawl slowly into the shell and subsist in repose. Johnny has left the sea shell behind, in the hands of the anima figure who gave it to him, for fun. He has transcended the parental "Omar Khayyam complex." He has gone on to dream in his element, water, and the reader may well surmise that the real hero of the story is the doctor, who must have known that a child who cannot imagine surely suffers a worse fate than one who can, no matter how ill, when he picked up the sea shell along the sounding shore.

SUSAN SPENCER

The Post-Apocalyptic Library: Oral and Literate Culture in Fahrenheit 451 and A Canticle for Leibowitz

At the dawn of widespread literacy in fourth-century Athens, Plato appended to the end of his *Phaedrus* a story that has often been perceived as, as Jacques Derrida puts it, "an extraneous mythological fantasy." Derrida argues in *Dissemination* that there is nothing extraneous about the myth at all, but rather it is an expression of an important and timely idea with which the classical Athenians were concerned. Recent orality/literacy theory, as outlined by Eric A. Havelock, Walter S. Ong, and others, would seem to back him up. The story is that of the discovery of the technology of writing, a tale that Socrates claims is traditional among the Egyptians. According to Socrates, the god Theuth invented this technology and offered it to the king of Upper Egypt as something that would "make the people of Egypt wiser and improve their memories." But the king scorned Theuth's gift, saying:

> by reason of your tender regard for the writing that is your offspring, [you] have declared the very opposite of its true effect. If men learn this, it will implant forgetfulness in their souls; they will cease to exercise memory because they rely on that which is written, calling things to remembrance no longer from within themselves, but by means of external marks. What you have discovered is a recipe not for memory, but for reminder. And it is

From *Extrapolation* 32, no. 4. © 1991 by Kent State University Press.

no true wisdom that you offer your disciples, but only its
semblance, for by telling them of many things without teaching
them you will make them seem to know much, while for the most
part they know nothing, and as men filled, not with wisdom, but
with the conceit of wisdom, they will be a burden to their fellows.

The remark about "telling them . . . without teaching them" is
evidently an expression of uneasiness with the idea of text as what Ong calls
"unresponsive." In *Orality and Literacy: The Technologizing of the Word*, Ong
sees one of Socrates's arguments as being "if you ask a person to explain his
or her statement, you can get an explanation; if you ask a text, you get back
nothing except the same, often stupid, words which called for your question
in the first place." While this idea is so commonplace to us as to go practically unnoticed, except when we are frustrated by a particularly opaque text,
it was new and frightening to the Greeks. According to Havelock in "The
Oral Composition of Greek Drama," the late fifth and early fourth century
B.C. was a period of relatively rapid change in literacy style, as a direct result
of the spread of popular literacy. Not only was an explanatory oral framework done away with, but also the old formulaic devices that helped oral
composers keep their place and remember what they were talking about.
"Compositionally, as plays began to be written with the expectation of being
read, the composer would feel a reduced pressure to conform to certain
mnemonic rules. The invented would be freer to prevail over the expected."
This, Havelock hypothesizes, created some tension in the Greek theater—a
tension that can be traced in Aristophanes's *Frogs*, where the more conservative, more "oral" Aeschylus wins a contest against the more "literary" and
startlingly original Euripides; and, as we can see (although Havelock does
not mention it here), in the inherent uneasiness in Plato's *Phaedrus*.

Although "The Oral Composition of Greek Drama" was first
published in 1980, some theory of postliterary tension was working its way
into the intelligentsia several decades before. To quote Havelock again, in his
1950 book *The Crucifixion of Intellectual Man*, the myth of the Fall in Genesis,
as a direct result of eating of the tree of knowledge, "gives poignant expression to that conflict within the civilized consciousness of man, between his
sense of intellectual power and his distrust and fear of that power. . . . All the
warmth and the richness of man's nature demand that he live in the protection of certain illusions in order to be secure, happy, and peaceful." The
"expected" rather than the "invented." The further the artificial "memory"
created by textuality stretches back, and the more it can be built upon by an
advancing science, the more that security fades away. Man becomes
dangerous and also frightened. "Though our science may kill us, it will never

allow us to retreat. Somehow we know that we would never burn enough books, nor eliminate enough intellectuals, to be able to return to the warm room" of blissful ignorance.

Within a decade of this assurance, two famous science fiction novels appeared dealing with the very attempt that Havelock had just pronounced futile: Ray Bradbury's *Fahrenheit 451* (1953) and Walter M. Miller's *A Canticle for Leibowitz* (1959). In *Fahrenheit 451* the protagonist, Guy Montag, is a "fireman"; that is, he burns forbidden books, and the houses that hide them, for a living. This is a busy job, considering the fact that just about all books are forbidden. There are a few rare exceptions, such as three-dimensional comic books, trade journals and, of course, rule books, those mainstays of any oppressive society. The rule book for the Firemen of America includes a brief history of the profession: "Established 1790, to burn English-influenced books in the Colonies. First Fireman: Benjamin Franklin." According to the only available text, and to the voice of political authority, this is a glorious and time-honored profession, an idea that gives the firemen a sense of continuity and security . . . and, perhaps, allows Bradbury to make a comment on the fact that textual knowledge is power, even—or perhaps especially—false knowledge. Power becomes unbreachable if textual information is monolithic. According to the sinister but brilliant fire chief, Beatty, the main danger in books is that "none of those books agree with each other." Very true, but a danger to whom? Peace of mind, he argues repeatedly. To one lawbreaker, kneeling despairingly amid her kerosene-soaked illegal books, Beatty cries, "You've been locked up here for years with a regular damned Tower of Babel. Snap out of it!"

Inevitably, Montag becomes discontented with the status quo and curious about this nebulous "danger." But his discontent and his curiosity are intensified when the woman mentioned above chooses to burn with her books rather than lose them. Beatty, seeing his distress when Montag feels "sick" and feigns illness, explains the real advent of the firemen in phrases that echo Havelock's concept of the loss of the "warm room" but takes it to its extreme limit:

> You always dread the unfamiliar. . . . We must all be alike. Not everyone born free and equal, as the Constitution says, but everyone *made* equal. Each man the image of every other; then all are happy, for there are no mountains to make them cower, to judge themselves against.

On the literary side, he also echoes Plato on the "conceit of wisdom," and just how far that can be taken as a sort of leveling device:

Give the people contests they win by remembering the words
to more popular songs or the names of state capitals or how
much corn Iowa grew last year. Cram them full of noncombustible data, chock them so damned full of 'facts' they feel
stuffed, but absolutely 'brilliant' with information. Then they'll
feel they're thinking, they'll get a *sense* of motion without
moving. And they'll be happy, because facts of that sort don't
change. Don't give them any slippery stuff like philosophy or
sociology to tie things up with. That way lies melancholy.

These things are written, but they are not literature. The classicist may
be reminded here of the problems associated with Linear B, the proto-Greek
script found at Mycenae and Knossos. All of the inscriptions are "bald
counting-house dockets," ⟨writes Leonard Palmer in *Myceneans and Minoans:
Aegean Prehistory in the Light of the Linear B Tablets* (1982)⟩, "a text of the
greatest interest" being a tablet that "lists amounts of barley against various
classes of craftsmen." There is no literature *per se*, unless one were to use the
standard eighteenth-century definition of literature as "anything written." As
a result, it is difficult to get students interested in learning Linear B. There
is simply nothing interesting to read. The situation is described by Havelock
as one of preliteracy, in spite of the physical existence of written text:
"whereas historians who have touched upon literacy as a historical phenomenon have commonly measured its progress in terms of the history of
writing, the actual conditions of literacy depend upon the history not of
writing but of reading." One needs an audience. Get the audience to lose
interest, and you can do away with the literate civilization. In *Fahrenheit 451*
the reader has the feeling of moving backward in time to a preliterate society,
and the content of the society's "literature," although here it is for political
ends, strengthens this impression.

The last phrase of Beatty's pronouncement, "That way lies melancholy," with its literary overtones—very different from the plainer common
speech of his subordinates—is not unusual for Beatty. In keeping with the
idea that knowledge is power, Bradbury gives us several hints that the fire
chief has had frequent access to the forbidden texts and that this is either a
cause or a result of his being made chief (just which one is unclear). Like
Kurt Vonnegut, Jr.'s short story "Harrison Bergeron," set in another
disturbing dystopia where "everybody [is] finally equal," some people are
seen clearly to be more equal than others and thus enabled to wield power
over their fellows. In Vonnegut's story, the ascendancy is physical: Diana
Moon Glampers, the "Handicapper General," is the only citizen who isn't
decked out in distorting glasses, distracting ear transmitters, and bags of

birdshot to weaken her to the level of society's lowest common denominator. In *Fahrenheit 451*, the ascendancy is purely textual, but that is enough. Beatty's obnoxious confidence and habit of quoting famous works strikes the reader immediately and leads to a question that Bradbury never answers: why is this highly literate person permitted to survive, let alone hold a position of high authority, in an aggressively oral society? Something is rotten in the whole system. Evidently someone higher up, Beatty's shadowy superior, feels that there is some inherent value in a well-read man, in spite of all the political rhetoric. This probability is directly opposed to Beatty's frequent deprecation of texts (a protection of his own monopoly?) and claim that the eventual ban of almost all books was not a political coup accomplished by a power-hungry elite at one fell swoop. Beatty's explanation, which we are never called upon to doubt, is that an outraged people seeking complete equality called for more and more censorship as texts became more widely available to interest groups that might be offended by them: "It didn't come from the Government down. There was no dictum, no declaration, no censorship, to start with, no! Technology, mass exploitation, and minority pressure carried the trick." As Plato warned thousands of years earlier, well-read man had become an offensive "burden to his fellows."

Bradbury closes the novel, however, with an optimistic view: the text *will* prevail, and man will be the better for it. This is shown symbolically in the escape from the city by Montag and Faber, the only two literate men in the story besides Beatty—who, also symbolically, perishes in the same manner as the many books he has burned. The ignorant oral-culture citizens, radios tamped securely in their ears, remain in the city to be blown up by an enemy they could easily have escaped, if it weren't for the fact that their monolithic media preferred to keep them ignorant and happy. Having taken up with a group of itinerant professors, haltingly trying to remember the text of Ecclesiastes, Montag takes the first steps toward realizing the dream he had as he blindly fled the government's persecution: "Somewhere the saving and the putting away had to begin again and someone had to do the saving and keeping, one way or another, in books, in records, in people's heads, any way at all so long as it was safe, free from moths, silverfish, rust and dry-rot, and men with matches."

The idea that it is safe only when locked away in memory is almost a startling one in this book that so privileges the literary text; it seems as if the author has come full circle to an oral culture and the need to circumvent the shortcomings of Theuth's invention. Yet Bradbury makes it clear that they will write everything down as soon as possible and will try to reconstruct a fully literate society again. This should not take long, and is certainly desirable. The concept of text is a progressive thing, not a cyclical, and as long as any remnants remain there is always a base, however small, on which to build a better and wiser world.

A far more ambiguous view is present in *A Canticle for Leibowitz*. The loss of literacy here is not a gradual, internal thing, but a reactionary disruption. The survivors of nuclear war, emerging from their fallout shelters to face a devastated world and irreversible chromosome damage, realize that they have been shut out of Havelock's "warm room" for good. And they're angry. So, like Bradbury's people, they seek comfort and revenge by destroying all texts and all individuals connected with learning, escaping into a simple agrarian lifestyle very different from Bradbury's high-tech nightmare. One technician, Isaac Leibowitz, escapes, and hides among a group of Cistercian monks with a contraband collection of written material he has managed to save from the general purge. Eventually he is found out by the mob and martyred. But the texts, without him as interpreter, survive and are handed down from generation to generation. As Leibowitz takes on the trappings of sainthood, the texts become holy items—not for what they communicate, but for what they *are*, something he died to protect. The collection is eclectic: half a physics book here, three charred pages of mathematical equations there, an old book of fairy tales—anything the monks can get their hands on. For centuries these are passed down, their meaning becoming obscured, and this is where Miller's narrative begins.

The novel is set up in three sections, each set six hundred years apart from its predecessor. The first, postulating a civilization very like the European Dark Ages, deals with a novice named Brother Francis, who inadvertently discovers some new texts in an ancient fallout shelter six centuries after what the new scriptures refer to as the second, or Flame, Deluge (to distinguish it from Noah's flood). The characters in part 1 are innocent and superstitious, very like the civilization that spawned such works as Caedmon's hymn (which is often read as an allegory for the literate Christian world superseding the oral world of the pre-Christian, preliterate "heathens"). The choice of Cistercians is an appropriate one: not only does it associate the Abbey of the Blessed Leibowitz with Monte Cassino, that similar repository of learning and text, but ⟨as Brian Stock writes in *The Implications of Literacy* (1983)⟩ "the organizational principles of movements like the Cistercians [in the middle ages] were clearly based on texts . . . Within the movement, texts were steps . . . by which the individual climbed toward a perfection thought to represent complete understanding and effortless communication with God."

As Brian Stock points out, "one of the clearest signs that a group had passed the threshold of literacy was the lack of necessity for the organizing text to be spelt out, interpreted, or reiterated." Brother Francis has not yet reached this level. In fact, Miller uses this lack of sophistication to humorous effect, showing how the monks have created a new oral mythos around the limited literature they have. When Francis discovers the fallout shelter (Maximum Occupancy: 15), he has enough literacy to read, but not to correctly interpret, the sign that identifies it:

> were not the monsters of the world still called "children of the Fallout"? That the demon was capable of inflicting all the woes which descended upon Job was a recorded fact . . . [and] he had unwittingly broken into the abode (deserted he prayed) of not just one, but fifteen of the dreadful beings!

The misinterpretation of the word "shelter" to mean a shelter *for*, rather than a shelter *from*, makes perfect grammatical sense. There is nothing wrong with Francis's reasoning, other than the fact that, as a semiotic critic would say, his sign system has broken down. When Francis runs into a similar problem over a memo reading, inexplicably, "Pound pastrami . . . can kraut, six bagels," the monks' painstakingly reconstructed "literacy" turns out to be a world of signifiers with no corresponding signifieds to give them concrete meaning. Words have truly been reduced to phonemes, units of sound; the morphological substructure is incomplete and inappropriate.

The papers in the shelter bear the name of I. A. Leibowitz, and, as relics, focus attention on the literary Memorabilia of a past era. The Blessed Leibowitz is canonized and so, in a way, are the newfound papers: they are incorporated into the canon of the Memorabilia, to be copied by generations of monks who do not always understand what they are copying. Brother Francis, for instance, spends fifteen years producing a gorgeous illuminated and gold-leafed copy of the blueprint for a circuit board, and literally gives his life for it in a world where there has been no humanly generated electricity for six hundred years. The fact that he begins by questioning the possible sacrilege of copying the original backwards (black on white rather than white on black) and is later relieved of his anxiety when he finds a fragment explaining blueprints and realizes that since "the color scheme of the blueprints was an accidental feature of those ancient drawings . . . [a] glorified copy of the Leibowitz print could be made without incorporating the accidental feature" is an additional semiotic joke on Miller's part. As they are copied, original documents are stored carefully away in lead-sealed, airtight casks, and faithful copies are made of the copies—with, of course, the occasional inevitable scribal mistake to provide a basis for future textual criticism.

Six hundred years after Brother Francis's discovery, the Abbey is still conducting itself along the same preliterate lines. Some advances in learning have been made, but not much of a practical nature. Although the naïveté is gone, it is still largely a case of learning solely for the disinterested sake of learning. There is a faint rumor of political conflict, but Hannegan, a local prince of Caesar-like ambition, is cheerfully illiterate and unlikely to show any interest in such an isolated area. This man has a literate cousin, however, who is very interested, indeed. Thon Taddeo receives permission to study the Memorabilia, and his "rediscovery" and interpretation of these hidden works prompts a renaissance of learning.

This is not altogether a good thing. The first indications of a theme of antiliteracy are, perhaps, in the portrayal of the character of the Poet who has taken up residence in the Abbey. He is crude and ill-mannered, a trial to the monks' calm and ritualistic existence. In this way he is very like poetry itself—that is, lyric poetry of the sort that reached its apex of popularity in our own Victorian period. One may recall John Stuart Mill's distinction between (mere) eloquence and poetry: "eloquence is *heard*; poetry is *over*heard." The Poet is definitely of the *over*heard variety: "The Poet has always muttered," complains the prior. He is a highly literate character, as unpredictable and inventive—and despised—as Aristophanes's Euripides. Not too surprisingly, the only book that is mentioned in the entire novel as being read for pleasure is a book of "daring" verses that the abbot in part 3 pulls out, a book said to be written by "Saint Poet of the Miraculous Eyeball," a reference to the Poet's glass eye. One might note that in part 3, when the world has become fully literate, the Poet is venerated as a saint, while in the semiliterate culture of part 2 he is regarded with mistrust and even dislike, for the most part. Marshall McLuhan identifies a similar mistrust in Pope's *Dunciad*, written at a period of increased circulation, and thus an increased reading audience, resulting in a stream of "self-indulgent" emotional poetry with no didactic purpose. He claims that "Book III [of the *Dunciad*] concerns the collective unconscious, the growing backwash from the tidal wave of self-expression. . . . Wit, the quick interplay among our senses and faculties, is thus steadily anaesthetized by the encroaching unconscious." A similar annihilation occurs with the loss of the socially instructive function of poetry, the direct descendant of preliterate eras when Achilles and Agamemnon and Jesus Christ were presented as patterns for behavior.

In part 2 of *Canticle*, books are still either to be copied in the scriptorium or read aloud at communal meals (which, perhaps significantly, the Poet does not generally attend). Upon Thon Taddeo's arrival he is treated to a reading aloud of a scriptural account of the Flame Deluge, in highly ritualistic style: "But one of the magi was like unto Judas Iscariot, and his testimony was crafty, and having betrayed his brothers, he lied to all the people, advising them not to fear the demon Fallout." The lesson contains a number of veiled warnings against the hubris of learning and the misuse of power, but Taddeo sweeps them all aside, disregarding everything but the archaic oralist language. He dismisses the warning as quaint, and heads for the library even as his retinue of soldiers begin sketching the Abbey's fortifications to report back to Hannegan its usefulness as a potential fortress—an action even more chilling when we consider it in the light of our own ill-conceived assault on Monte Cassino in 1944, a raid in which Miller took part and which was the partial genesis of *A Canticle for Leibowitz*. This secular influx, it is clear, bodes no good for the store of learning. A further note of foreboding is sounded when the Poet quits the monastery, leaving his glass eye with Taddeo: the abbot explains that as he was in the habit of removing the eye whenever he was about to do something outrageous, the brothers and the Poet himself have come to refer to the eye as "the Poet's conscience." Taddeo replies, "So he thinks I need it more than he does."

There are other parallels with our own literary history that come out in part 2, although Miller reverses the traditional role of the church vs. secular forces. Even as it is not writing, but reading, that defines a literate culture, in many ways it isn't so much writing, but *not*-writing, that is the political act. In a conference paper in 1981, Ong pointed out that "the totality of existence-saturated time is simply too much to manage." The author has to pick and choose, simply by nature of his medium. Ong illustrates this with a quotation from the book of John: "There are still many other things that Jesus did, yet if they were written about in detail, I doubt there would be room enough in the entire world to hold the books to record them" (21:25). In this case, the choice is clear: "the author picks from Jesus's life what is particularly relevant to human beings' salvation." The issue of what gets preserved is a similar one. Jeff Opland reminds us in his book on *Anglo Saxon Oral Poetry* that much of what is reported about poetry, and what poetry we have, is inextricably tied up with church politics and what the Catholic Church deemed worthy of preservation. Basically, it comes down to a situation of who has the vellum.

The extreme of this is, of course, Orwell's *1984*, but it is also an aspect of preliteracy. The Sapir-Whorf hypothesis—the idea that our language shapes our perceptions of reality—is most easily observed in preliterate cultures. Their values, their thought, and even their vocabulary is much more homogeneous: "Sapir-Whorfian notions of cultural relativity in distinctions encoded within differing languages apply more obviously to cultures which have remained primarily oral . . . since oral cultures, lacking dictionaries, delete from the lexicon as well as create distinctions within it according to the criterion of current social usefulness" (writes Alan Durant).

Miller's monks are aware of this in a subconscious sort of way, and attempt to maintain a homogeneity of cherishing everything equally. To them, all texts are holy, and they continue to treasure their illuminated grocery lists long after they have grown sophisticated enough to realize that these texts are likely to be of doubtful utility. Text is above utility or politics and has entered the realm of the sacred, taking on almost the mystic quality of runes, or the writing on a well-known Greek cup dating back to preliterate days: "Whoso drinks this drinking cup straightway him / Desire shall seize of fair-crowned Aphrodite." Writing itself has the power, rather than the person who exploits it. Taddeo never realizes this. Even as he travels toward the Abbey he explains to the nomad tribes which are providing him with an escort that he is seeking "*incantations* of great power" (italics are Miller's) that will be of tactical use for him.

By not giving privilege to any particular genre or subject, the monks have effectively depoliticized the medium, a situation that comes to an abrupt end when Taddeo comes along to make distinctions between what is useful and what is not. Thus Taddeo's rediscovery of the Memorabilia is not just a renaissance of science but also a revolution in the role of text as communication rather than text as object. The change in role is not accomplished without some trepidation on the part of the more conservative monks, in particular the librarian: "To the custodian of the Memorabilia, each unsealing represented another decrease in the probable lifetime of the contents of the cask, and he made no attempt to conceal his disapproval of the entire proceeding. To Brother Librarian, whose task in life was the preservation of books, the principal reason for the existence of books was that they might be preserved perpetually."

The librarian is the extreme case, but even the abbot is concerned about such an abrupt and complete dissemination of texts, as he confides to Taddeo in one of the most important passages in the book:

> You promise to begin restoring Man's control over Nature. But who will govern the use of the power to control natural forces? Who will use it? To what end? Such decisions can still be made. But if you and your group don't make them now, others will soon make them for you. Mankind will profit, you say. By whose sufferance? The sufferance of a prince who signs his letters X?

This is the turning point. As Alan Durant remarks, "literacy leads to a diversification of, and contradictions within, previously homogeneous 'oral' cultures, as readers are differentially influenced by earlier stages of the cultural record, interpret them differently, and use them to support divergent versions of aspiration and intent." This is what Beatty was warning of in

Fahrenheit 451, and now it is what Thon Taddeo opens up. When the abbot pleads with him to slow down his investigations and keep destructive information out of Hannegan's hands, Taddeo characteristically misinterprets him and believes that he is forcing religion down his throat. "'Would you have me work for the Church?' The scorn in his voice was unmistakable."

As a result of Taddeo's reintroduction of the Memorabilia to the general public, six centuries later "there were spaceships again" and electric lights and newspapers and all manner of technological marvels. When we first meet the third and final abbot he is being held at bay by an "Abominable Autoscribe," a machine that converts oral text to written (and, if necessary, into a foreign language, to boot). The fact that it doesn't work is indicative of the difficulties of all writing: having lost the ability to communicate orally—the abbot is trying to write a letter to a cardinal who doesn't speak his language—he finds himself at the mercy of an imperfect technology. Yet he admits that "I don't trust my own Anglo-Latin, and if I did, *he'd* probably not trust his." As Socrates's King of Egypt predicted, the medium that was meant to increase memory has actually decreased it, with potentially disastrous results: the aborted letter was a request for orders concerning Operation Peregrinatur, a plan to evacuate selected members of the Order to the off-world colonies on Alpha Centauri, since it has become obvious that history has repeated itself and mankind is once again manufacturing nuclear weapons.

Inevitably, war does come and the Operation is put into effect. Having lost their function as guardians of the Memorabilia, the monks spend all of part 3 desperately trying to escape its effects. As "the visage of Lucifer mushroom[s] into hideousness above the cloudbank, rising slowly like some titan climbing to its feet after ages of imprisonment in the Earth," the starship lifts into the sky with a cargo of twenty-seven monks, six nuns, twenty children . . . and the Memorabilia, preserved *in toto* on microfilm. "It was no curse, this knowledge, unless perverted by Man, as fire had been, this night." But of course it will be, eventually. Text, with the seeds of destruction encoded within it, follows Man like a recurring damnation. Man, the textual animal, will Deconstruct the universe.

Both *A Canticle for Leibowitz* and *Fahrenheit 451* end with a nuclear apocalypse and a new literacy springing from the ashes. Bradbury's positive, progressive view of literary history contrasts sharply with Miller's negative, cyclical view, just as Bradbury's depiction of a predominately oral culture as mind-numbing contrasts with Miller's depiction of orality as the preserver of ritual and collective human values. One might conclude this paper with the Unanswerable Question so popular with medieval bards at the ends of their stories: "Which point of view is the correct one?" And, as it has always been, the correct answer is "both."

DAVID SEED

The Flight from the Good Life: Fahrenheit 451 in the Context of Postwar American Dystopias

Surveying the American scene in 1958, Aldous Huxley recorded his dismay over the speed with which *Brave New World* was becoming realized in contemporary developments: "The nightmare of total organization, which I had situated in the seventh century After Ford, has emerged from the safe, remote future and is now awaiting us, just around the next corner." Having struck a keynote of urgency Huxley then lines up a series of oppositions between limited disorder, individuality and freedom on the one hand, and order, automatism and subjection on the other in order to express his liberal anxieties that political and social organization might hypertrophy. Huxley sums up an abiding fear which runs through American dystopian fiction of the 1950s that individuals will lose their identity and become the two-dimensional stereotypes indicated in two catch-phrases of the period: the "organization man" and the "man in the grey flannel suit." William H. Whyte's 1956 study diagnoses the demise of the Protestant ethic in American life and its replacement by a corporate one which privileges "belongingness." The result might be, he warns, not a world controlled by self-evident enemies familiar from *Nineteen Eighty-Four*, but an antiseptic regime presided over by a "mild-looking group of therapists who, like the Grand Inquisitor, would be doing what they did to help you." Whyte endorsed the social insights of Sloan Wilson's 1955 novel *The Man in the Grey Flannel Suit* which dramatizes the

From *Journal of American Studies* 28, no. 2. © 1994 Cambridge University Press.

conflicts within the protagonist between individual advancement and self-location within a business hierarchy. Despite being an apparently successful executive Thomas Rath registers a tension between satisfaction and its opposite which recurs throughout fifties dystopias.

One crucial sign of this issue is the fact that the protagonists of dystopias are usually defined in relation to organizational structures. Walter M. Miller's 1952 short story "Conditionally Human" is typical of the genre in centering on an official. The action takes place in an America of the near future which has become "one sprawling suburb" ruled over by "Uncle Federal." Because the inexorable rise in the population is clearly threatening the promise of the "good life" the regime introduces draconian limits to the birth rate and the government-sponsored organization Anthropos Inc. designs baby substitutes called "neutroids," chimp-like creatures produced by the radioactive mutation of reproductive cells. The central character Norris has the job of an updated dog-catcher, rounding up stray "neutroids" to his wife's disgust. Already we can see the key generic motifs emerging: the problem of homogeneity, the disparity between restriction and avuncular government, the risk of technology exceeding its moral bounds, and—within the Norris couple—the debate between acceptance and dissatisfaction. When questioned by his wife, Norris characteristically pleads helplessness by appealing to the necessities of the system: "And what can I do about it? I can't help my Placement Aptitude score. They say Bio-Authority is where I belong, and it's to Bio I have to go. Oh, sure, I don't *have* to work where they send me. You can always join the General Work Pool, but that's all the law allows, and GWP'ers don't have families. So I go where Placement Aptitude says I'm needed." Psychometrics has become institutionalized into a narrow series of legally enforced prescriptions which induce an acquiescence in Norris reflected in the key verb "belongs."

The adjustment of the individual's notion of appropriateness to officially measured norms evident in the story just quoted also figured prominently in the sociologist Mordecai Roshwald's examination of American society in the late fifties. Viewing developments with the special clarity of a newcomer (Roshwald was born in Poland and lived in Palestine before he took up permanent residence in the USA), he applied David Riesman's notion of other-directedness and located a resultant tendency to "imitation and uniformity." His 1958 article "Quo Vadis, America?" concludes with an indignant polemic against the complacency of imagining that the only danger confronting society is the external physical threat of atomic war. Not so. "The loss of individual norms in moral issues, the admiration of unjust power, the lack of tradition" and a host of other dangers present themselves just as urgently, and Roshwald here opens up a potential purpose for the writer of dystopias: "to warn against these and to fight them may be a second front in the fight for human survival. . . ." Roshwald was in fact already contributing to that fight by working on his own dystopian novel *Level 7* (1959) which transposed the streamlined production systems of *Brave New World* on to the self-contained mechanized environment of a nuclear defence bunker. The inordinate reliance on technology and bland interchangeability of American manners which "seemed to point to a uniformly happy, efficient and self-sufficient society, verging on automata or robots," finds its expression in the novel as an ironic implication that the operative-protagonist is an extension of his machines instead of vice versa. As happens with Montag in *Fahrenheit 451*, X-127, known only by his functional label, comes gradually to realize the consequences of his participation in a system, here of nuclear destruction, but with the added irony that his realization comes too late to make any difference even to his own fate. Roshwald's original title for this work was *The Diary of Push-Button Officer X-127* which appropriately stressed the issue of robotization, partly problematizing the individual's relation to technology and partly using that technology as a metaphorical expression of the individual's conformity to prescribed roles. Quite independently Erich Fromm identified the emergence of exactly the same social type, declaring: "Today we come across a person who acts and feels like an automaton; who never experiences anything which is really his; who experiences himself entirely as the person he thinks he is supposed to be."

Ray Bradbury's *Fahrenheit 451* (1953) goes one step further. Not only is the protagonist Montag initially a robot too, he is also a member of the state apparatus which enforces such prescriptions by destroying the books which might counteract the solicitations of the media. The regime of the novel masks its totalitarianism with a façade of material prosperity. Montag's superior Beatty explains its coming-into-being as a benign process of inevitable development, everything being justified on the utilitarian grounds of the majority's happiness: "technology, mass exploitation, and minority pressure carried the trick, thank God." A levelling-down is presented as a triumph of technological know-how and of system; above all it was a spontaneous transformation of society not a dictatorial imposition ("it didn't come from the Government down"). Bradbury's description of the media draws on *Brave New World* as confirmed by postwar developments in television. Observing the latter boom in America, Huxley commented: "In *Brave New World* non-stop distractions of the most fascinating nature . . . are deliberately used as instruments of policy, for the purpose of preventing people from paying too much attention to the realities of the social and political situation." He continues in terms directly relevant to the world of Bradbury's

novel: "A society, most of whose members spend a great deal of their time
. . . in the irrelevant other worlds of sport and soap opera . . . will find it hard
to resist the encroachments of those who would manipulate and control it."
Where Beatty minimizes the firemen's role as benevolent guardians of the
status quo, Huxley refuses such a tendentiously spontaneous account in order
to pinpoint political purpose.

The result of this process in *Fahrenheit 451* is a consumer culture
completely divorced from political awareness. An aural refrain running
through the novel is the din of passing bombers which has simply become
background noise. This suggests a total separation of political action from
everyday social life and correspondingly when Montag's wife Millie and her
friends agree to "talk politics" the discussion revolves entirely around the
names and appearances of the figures concerned. In other words the latter
have become images within a culture dominated by television. "The
Fireman" (the first version of *Fahrenheit 451*) summarizes the typical
programmes as follows:

> . . . there on the screen was a man selling orange soda pop and a
> woman drinking it with a smile; how could she drink and smile
> simultaneously? A real stunt! Following this, a demonstration of
> how to bake a certain new cake, followed by a rather dreary
> domestic comedy, a news analysis that did not analyze anything
> and did not mention the war, even though the house was shaking
> constantly with the flight of new jets from four directions, and an
> intolerable quiz show naming state capitals.

The very tempo of this list, a rapid sequence of short items, has been
explained by Beatty as economy ("the centrifuge flings off all unnecessary,
time-wasting thought") but the discourse of production has now become
contradictory as it has been displaced onto consumption. If commercial efficiency notionally releases workers to enjoy new leisure opportunities, the
aim of the new media is to fill that leisure time not to economize on it.

The novel significantly magnifies the references to TV which occur in
"The Fireman" on to a larger scale. Montag's living room has become a 3-D
televisual environment for his wife who dreams of adding a fourth wall-
screen so that the house will seem no longer theirs but "exotic people's." One
of Montag's earliest realizations in the novel is that his house is exactly like
thousands of others. Identical and therefore capable of substitution, it can
never be his own. That is why the clichéd designation by the media of Millie
as "homemaker" is so absurdly ironic because at the very moment when the
television is promoting one role it is also feeding her with desires which push

in the opposite direction, ultimately inviting her to identify with another place preferable to her more mundane present house. *Fahrenheit 451* dramatizes the effects of the media as substitutions. Millie finds an ersatz intimacy with the "family" on the screen which contrasts markedly with her relation to Montag. Again and again the dark space of their bedroom is stressed, its coldness and silence; whereas Millie's favourite soap operas keep up a constant hubbub and medley of bright colours.

Millie and her friends are defined entirely by their roles as consumers, whether of sedatives, soap-operas, or fast cars. Bradbury anticipates Marshall McLuhan by presenting the media which stimulate this consumption as extensions of faculties (the thimble anticipations of Walkmans) or their substitutes (the toaster has hands to save her the trouble of touching the bread). A bizarre passage Bradbury planned to include in the novel pushes the dehumanizing effects of the media to Gothic extremes:

> They sat in the room with the little electronic vampires feeding silently at their throats, touching at their jugulars with great secretness. Their faces were masked over with black velvet, and their bodies were draped in such a way as not to prove whether man or woman sat there beneath. And the hands were gloved with thickened, sexless material, and only the faintest gleam showed in the slits of their eyes, in the half dark twilight room.

Here dress performs a near total erasure of feature and even gender, replacing skin with an insulating patina. Bradbury's application of the vampire myth stresses loss of vitality whereas Marshall McLuhan draws on the story of Narcissus: "This extension of himself by mirror numbed his perceptions until he became the servomechanism of his own extended or repeated image." The result in both cases is immobility and the creation of a closed system between the individual and technology which, in the Bradbury passage quoted above, drains off the sociability of the gathering described. Mildred's house combines all the electronic gadgetry associated with the fifties "good life." But these things have a cost. Bradbury further anticipates McLuhan in rendering television as an aggressive medium: "Music bombarded him at such an immense volume that his bones were almost shaken from his tendons," and then, as it quietens down, "you had the impression that someone had turned on a washing-machine or sucked you up in a gigantic vacuum." The experience of one consumable can only be understood through comparison with another, and here the individual is put into a posture of maximum passivity as subjected to machines, not their controller. McLuhan explains the television in far more positive terms, but still ones which partly echo Bradbury's. Thus "with TV, the viewer is the screen. He is bombarded with light impulses." And because TV is no good for background it makes more demands on the viewer than does radio: "Because the low definition of TV insures a high degree of audience involvement, the most effective programs are those that present situations which consist of some process to be completed." Bradbury burlesques this notion of audience participation as no more than an electronic trick whereby an individual's name can be inserted into a gap in the announcer's script (and even his lip-movements adjusted).

The media in Bradbury's novel then induce a kind of narcosis. There is both a continuity and an analogy between Millie watching the wall-screens and then taking sleeping pills. Similarly in *Brave New World* the opiate soma has become the religion of the people. Huxley subsequently explained that "the soma habit was not a private vice; it was a political institution." Bradbury's emphasis on the consumer end of the cycle of production was shared by, for example, Ann Warren Griffith whose 1953 story "Captive Audience" portrays an America dominated by the Master Ventriloquism Corporation which specializes in placing aural advertisements in consumables. The Corporation's influence on Congress and the Supreme Court has been so successful that any resistance to their sales techniques has been declared illegal. The writer who most successfully dramatized the political power of business combines in this period was however Frederik Pohl. His collaboration with Cyril Kornbluth, *The Space Merchants* (1953), rewrites the Cold War across a commercial grid. The world has been almost taken over by a massive American-based multinational named Schocken Associates which is locked into a struggle with its main rival, not only for the world market but also to develop Venus commercially. Working against Schocken is an organization of subversive Conservationists known as "Consies." Mitchell Courtenay functions happily as an advertising executive within Schocken until a complex series of events displace him into the alien contexts at the opposite extremes of the social spectrum, so that he experiences a series of discoveries about the nature of manual labour and consumerism. It is the impetus of the plot itself which carries Courtenay towards social awareness and therefore towards disenchantment with his company, whereas we shall see that Montag's flight from his culture is more willed.

The essential trigger to that flight is supplied by an alienation not only from suburban monotony but also from Montag's consumer-wife. He contemplates her as if she has ceased to be a human being: ". . . he saw her without opening his eyes, her hair burnt by chemicals to a brittle straw, her eyes with a kind of cataract unseen but suspect far behind the pupils, the reddened pouting lips, the body as thin as a praying mantis from dieting, and her flesh like white bacon." Millie here fragments into disparate features transformed by dye, cosmetics or dieting. Instead of being the consumer she is now consumed by commercially induced processes. The passage points backwards to an original state which is no longer recoverable and in that respect the images approach the free-floating state of simulation described by Jean Baudrillard. In the contemporary phase of capitalism, he argues, abstraction and simulation now involve the "generation by models of a real **without origin or reality: a hyperreal." Signs now become substitutions for the real, at their most extreme bearing no relation to any reality.** It is the penultimate phase of the image or sign, however, which best glosses Bradbury's novel, namely when the image "masks the *absence* of a basic reality" (Baudrillard's emphasis). The adjective "reddened" only appears to suggest a physical state prior to make-up. Later in the novel when Millie flees from the house without lipstick her mouth is simply "gone," as if the adjective has grotesquely taken over actuality from its referent.

Montag clearly functions as a satirical means for Bradbury to question the impetus of consumerism and passages like the one just quoted estrange Montag from an environment he has been taking for granted. Frederik Pohl likewise exploits estrangement effects in "The Tunnel under the World" (1954). Here the executive-protagonist goes to the office on what seems to be a perfectly normal morning, normal that is until small differences begin to strike him like the fact that he is offered a new brand of cigarettes. Guy Burckhardt's routine, even his sense of reality, has been determined by an accumulation of such details: brand names, consumer objects, and advertising jingles. To his understandable horror Burckhardt discovers that a local company Contro (control?) Chemicals has concealed a massive industrial accident by building a replica of his town and has even housed the brains of the few survivors—Burckhardt's included—in anthropoid robots. The story in other words presents a grim parable of the extent to which commerce can construct the consumer's reality, appropriately reflecting Kingsley Amis's claim that Pohl's characteristic work is the "satirical utopia."

Where Pohl briefly surveys the control of a whole environment Bradbury sets up contrasts between different kinds of social space in *Fahrenheit 451*, particularly between interiors and exteriors. A 1951 short story, "The Pedestrian," anticipates these themes and describes a point of transition just before the uniformity of the novel is finally established. The subject is simple: a pedestrian is arrested for walking the streets at night. The opening paragraph introduces an iterative account of what the protagonist has been doing for ten years:

> To enter out into that silence that was the city at eight o'clock of a misty evening in November, to put your feet upon that buckling concrete walk, step over grassy seams and make your way,

hands in pockets, through the silences, that was what Mr.
Leonard Mead most dearly loved to do. He would stand upon
the corner of an intersection and peer down long moonlit
avenues of sidewalk in four directions, deciding which way to go,
but it really made no difference; he was alone in this world of
2053 A.D. . . .

Bradbury's infinitives and then his use of the hypothetical second person
draw the reader into a pattern of action which turns out to be a rhetorical
cul-de-sac because Mead, it transpires, is the last of his line pursuing a
habit which has become obsolete. The unusual opening phrase destabi-
lizes our distinction between interior and exterior space and the description then draws on post-romantic survival narratives like Mary Shelley's
The Last Man to suggest an ultimate state of isolation. But Mead stands in
ironic proximity to a new species of citizens who, in anticipation of Millie,
fill their leisure time watching television. Even the police car which arrests
Mead (since there are no officers inside it is literally the car which does the
arresting) is the last of its line since there is no longer any urban crime,
and the story concludes with Mead being taken away to the "Psychiatric
Center for Research On Regressive Tendencies," thereby signalling the
demise of a social possibility. When Bradbury worked this story into his
novel it became part of the regime's past, helping to explain why in
Fahrenheit 451 the nocturnal streets are either deserted or used as impro-
vised race tracks.

It is of course a truism that the dystopias of the fifties base themselves
on the premise that dissatisfaction with the prevalent regime will be regis-
tered sooner or later by their protagonists. In order to accelerate this process
of realization some novelists use catalyst-figures whose role is to function as
a productive irritant in the protagonist's consciousness. So Clarisse, the niece
it turns out of Leonard Mead, fascinates and disturbs Montag because she
seems wilfully to stand outside social norms. Neither child nor woman, she
introduces herself as a social misfit ("I'm seventeen and I'm crazy") and challenges Montag to confront awkward questions such as whether he is happy.
In Kurt Vonnegut's *Player Piano* (also published temporarily under the title
Utopia 14) Finnerty also performs the role of misfit. He is an old friend of
Paul Proteus but his appalling manners repeatedly disrupt the decorum of
the rituals which bond together that novel's managerial elite. Like Montag
Proteus envies the apparent freedom of the other: "It was an appalling
thought, to be so well-integrated into the machinery of society and history
as to be able to move in only one plane, and along one line. Finnerty's arrival
was disturbing, for it brought to the surface the doubt that life should be that

way. Paul had been thinking of hiring a psychiatrist to make him docile, content with his lot, amiable to all." As in *Brave New World* the factory system once again sets coordinates for the self and Proteus feels himself to be tugged in two directions: On the one hand Finnerty lifts his level of dissatisfaction, on the other a psychiatrist—again a typical detail of the genre—would encourage acquiescence to the regime in the name of "adjustment."

Fahrenheit 451 and *Player Piano* both narrate a dual process of learning and disengagement where the protagonist's field of consciousness supplies the ground of the action, indeed even becomes the central issue within that action. At one·point Clarisse declares "this is the age of the disposable tissue," a strategic pun on Bradbury's part which relates directly to Vonnegut's novel also since both writers are describing acts of resistance towards social and economic systems where human beings have become dispensable material. Characters accordingly are grouped oppositionally around the protagonists. Finnerty's niggling influence on Proteus is counterbalanced by those representatives of his managerial group who warn him what he might lose. In *Fahrenheit 451* Clarisse and then later an English professor named Faber stimulate Montag towards overt resistance, whereas Beatty functions as antagonist. From a very early stage in the novel Montag internalizes Beatty's voice as a censorious or punitive force, the voice of the superego resisting taboo thoughts or actions. Every scene where Beatty figures then becomes charged with ambiguity as if he is accusing Montag of crimes. When the latter comes down with a "fever" Beatty visits him without being called, explaining that he could foresee what was going to happen. In a simulation of a doctor's visit Beatty tries to deindividualize Montag's problem as a typical case which will pass. If we visualize Montag being addressed on the one side by Beatty and on the other by Faber like a morality play, although the latter occupies the moral high ground, Beatty represents a far more sinister presence by his uncanny knack of predicting what Montag will think. Francois Truffaut described the action as "une forme de lutte contre l'autorité" and Montag must kill Beatty as the personification of that authority however euphemistically the latter presents his power.

The key progression in this process is a shift from the latent to the overt, from the implicit to the explicit. Montag discovers an inner voice which he has been suppressing and his previously unified self fractures into dissociations of mind from body and limb from limb: "His hands had been infected, and soon it would be his arms. He could feel the poison work up his wrists and into his elbows and his shoulders, and then the hump-over from shoulder-blade to shoulder-blade like a spark leaping a gap. His hands were ravenous. And his eyes were beginning to feel hunger. . . ." The metaphor of poison encodes Montag's dissidence within the ideology of a regime devoted to maintaining the so-called health of the body politic; but the displaced hunger of his other limbs suggests a desire that will take him out of that dominant ideology. We can see from this passage how the issue of authority pervades the very style of the novel. In his 1968 article "Death Warmed Over" Bradbury mounts a spirited defence of classic horror movies and fantasy fiction by contrasting two broad artistic methods: the accumulation of fact and the use of symbolism. He condemns the former as being appropriate to another discipline altogether: "We have fallen into the hands of the scientists, the reality people, the data collectors." And he goes on to propose selective resonance as an alternative. "The symbolic acts, not the miniscule details of the act, are everything." Retrospectively this article helps to explain the method of *Fahrenheit 451* which, like the other dystopias of the period, uses the dissatisfaction of one individual to reflect on the general inadequacies of a regime perceived as in some sense totalitarian. This dissatisfaction is articulated through an intricate series of symbols and images which support the action at every point. The repeated syntagmatic metaphors always run counter to the fixity and therefore the values of the official discourse of the state.

The most prominent example of such symbolism occurs in the references to fire. Donald Watt has argued that "burning as constructive energy, and burning as apocalyptic catastrophe, are the symbolic poles of Bradbury's novel" and certainly the antithesis of extremes could not be stronger between fire as destructive and fire as transforming or life-giving. The range of signification is introduced in the astonishing first paragraph of the novel:

> IT WAS A PLEASURE TO BURN.
> It was a special pleasure to see things eaten, to see things blackened and *changed*. With the brass nozzle in his fists, with this great python spitting its venomous kerosene upon the world, the blood pounded in his head, and his hands were the hands of some amazing conductor playing all the symphonies of blazing and burning to bring down the tatters and charcoal ruins of history. With his symbolic helmet numbered 451 on his stolid head, and his eyes all orange flame with the thought of what came next, he flicked the igniter and the house jumped up in a gorging fire that burned the evening sky red and yellow and black.

The opening sentence leaves an ambiguity about how active the verb is, suggesting at once an intransitive state which looks forward to Montag's "fever" of disobedience, and also suggesting an absent object. Although we know that Montag is a fireman the description shifts voice to place him in the position of a spectator rather than an agent. The true object of "burn" is deferred until Part III of the novel where Montag destroys first his house and then Beatty. Already the political theme of the regime's attempted erasure of the past has been established and also the quasi-sexual intoxication of power. The latter implication came out more strongly in Bradbury's original version of the passage where the third sentence read: "With his symbolic number 451 on his earnest head, with his eyes all orange fire with the very thought of what was to come, he let the boa-constrictor, the pulsing fire-hose in his fists spray the highly incandescent fluid upon the flanks of the ancient building." Here sex and work have become more firmly identified in a depiction of orgasmic destruction and the passage (in either version) articulates a preliminary state of mind where Montag is totally engrossed by his work. Questioning comes later.

Symbolism of course is historically determined and vulnerable to political manipulations and fire symbolism is no exception. On the night of 10 May, 1933, Nazi followers destroyed piles of books in German university towns. As the flames rose in the square opposite the University of Berlin the Propaganda Minister Dr. Goebbels praised the gathered throng for ending the "age of extreme jewish intellectualism" and ushering in the new German era: "From these ashes there will rise the phoenix of a new spirit . . . The past is lying in flames. The future will rise from the flames within our own hearts." The equivalent of such utterances in Bradbury's novel are slogan-like statements by Beatty ("fire is bright and fire is clean") but the symbolism has become even more rigidly codified in the uniforms and equipment of the firemen. It would be wrong to suggest any direct application by Bradbury of such historical occurrences because his novel does not explicitly identify the country being described. On the other hand, like Mordecai Roshwald in *Level 7*, he positions the reader so as to be able to infer connections with the USA. In a retrospective article on the novel Bradbury comments on the Nazi book-burning: "when Hitler burned a book I felt it as keenly, please forgive me, as his killing a human, for in the long sum of history they are one and the same flesh." And he has since confirmed that the main burnings he had in mind were those which took place in Soviet Russia and Nazi Germany, adding: "fortunately, nothing of the sort in the United States. Minor altercations with town censors, mayors, politicians, which have all blown away in the wind." In fact the situation in the United States was serious enough for the American Library Association to issue a manifesto in 1953, the same year as Bradbury's novel, which proclaimed that "the freedom to read is essential to our democracy" and which set out to protect exactly those rights which have disappeared in *Fahrenheit 451*:

> Private groups and public authorities in various parts of the
> country are working to remove books from sale, to censor text-
> books, to label "controversial" books, to distribute lists of
> "objectionable" books or authors and to purge libraries. These
> actions apparently rise from a view that our national tradition
> of free expression is no longer valid; that censorship and
> suppression are needed to avoid the subversion of politics and
> the corruption of morals.

The document rails against the encroaching power of officialdom to
prescribe taste which the "firemen" are doing without any constraint.

The state control of the printed word has been a major concern in
modern dystopias. Yevgeny Zamyatin's *We* describes the use of the *Gazette of
the One State* to induce the individual's subservience to collective civic
purposes ("the beauty of a mechanism lies in that which is undeviating and
exact"). *Brave New World* polarises literary expression between the minimal
expressive needs of the present and the library of "pornographic old books"
locked away in the safe of the Controller, himself a precursor of Beatty. And
Nineteen Eighty-Four collapses together "every conceivable kind of information, instruction, or entertainment" in the Records Department of the
Ministry of Truth so that newspapers, text books, and novels all function on
the same level of representation. In these three classic dystopias the state
reduces printed output to a utilitarian minimum, whether in the name of
political efficiency or the supposed happiness of the greatest number. By
depicting a regime where *all* books are banned, however, Bradbury impli-
cates the reader from the very start in illegality, in an oppositional relation to
the regime. Automatically then Montag's resistance becomes privileged as he
learns to cherish books, as he appropriates the official fire-symbolism to his
own purposes (reading it as suggestive of renewal), and most importantly as
he gradually refuses the state separation of books from humans. One draft for
the novel has Beatty describe the destruction of the former as an execution
("Books are dinosaurs, they were dying anyway. We just gave them the bullet
behind the ear"), whereas Bradbury has summed up the novel as revolving
round a "book-burner who suddenly discovers that books are flesh and
blood." What Bradbury draws our attention to here is the insistent series of
humanizing metaphors in his novel which revitalise books and which prevent
them from being regarded as inanimate objects.

The last part of *Fahrenheit 451* traces out the consequences of Montag's
estrangement from his society. His physical flight expresses in terms of action
a disengagement which has already taken place in his mind. Here again Bradbury is following a generic pattern. We have already noted the displacement

of the protagonist in *The Space Merchants*. Vonnegut's Paul Proteus also has
to transgress the boundaries of his city Ilium which have been erected to
separate personnel from machines, managerial elite from workers. Where
Proteus crosses a literal and metaphorical bridge between these domains
Montag undergoes a rite of passage which involves the death of his old self
(spuriously enacted on the TV by the authorities) and rebirth by water (the
crossing of a river). Just as the city of Ilium is destroyed in an attempted
putsch so Montag's city is laid waste by atomic bombing out of which
emerges a strange new beauty: "gouts of shattered concrete and sparkles of
torn metal" compose into a "mural hung like a reversed avalanche."

Both Bradbury and Vonnegut refute their regimes' claims of progress
by investing a special value in the past. The eponymous object which gives
Player Piano its title is a historical throwback to an earlier period and is also
a machine played by the ghost of a craftsmanship which has become obsolete. Proteus attempts to enact his disillusionment with modern automation
by taking possession of an old farmhouse but this solitary gesture proves to
be futile. Montag by contrast discovers a whole social group devoted to
preserving books through memory, thereby actualising Bradbury's earlier
metaphors of books-as-people. Similarly in Walter M. Miller's *A Canticle for
Leibowitz* (1959) a surviving remnant from a nuclear holocaust preserves the
few surviving books through "book-leggers" who smuggle them to safety or
through "memorizers." One critic has complained that the last section of
Bradbury's novel is "vague in political detail" but the national references are
clear and specific. The hoboes gathered round their campfires and constantly
moving on to avoid a threatening state authority recall the unemployed tran-
sients of the Depression (even the rusting railway line strengthens this echo).
And the leader of the campers is named after the Granger Movement which
flourished in the USA in the late 1860s and 1870s. This movement made a
collective protest against the encroachments of large-scale capitalism and
asserted the values of the local agrarian community. Its Declaration of
Purposes asserted the aim "to labor for the good of our Order, our Country,
and mankind"; and the movement set up reading programmes for farming
families among other measures. Although Montag rediscovers the communal
space of the campsite and although the campers do possess contemporary
technology, all the appeal of place and community lies in its appeal to the
past. Personal memory and collective history blur together as the novel
concludes with an attempted exercise in radical conservation which plays on
the reader's own historical memory of a lost agrarian past.

Concluding her 1957 survey of utopian thought from the Enlightenment through romantic despair and Christian fatalism Judith N. Shklar
pronounces what is in effect an obituary on the very notion of utopia: ". . .

radicalism in general has gone totally out of fashion. Radicalism is not the readiness to indulge in revolutionary violence; it is the belief that people can control and improve themselves and, collectively, their social environment. Without this minimum of utopian faith no radicalism is meaningful." While it is certainly true that fifties dystopias situate their protagonists in relation to regimes which have apparently concentrated power on a massive scale, the result is by no means simple acquiescence. These are works with as it were a double gaze on the reader's present and on the hypothetical future. As Vonnegut declares in his foreword to *Player Piano*, "this book is not a book about what is, but a book about what could be." The direction taken by social change is repeatedly depicted as an erasure of the known and it is here that a polemical edge emerges in the dystopias.

KEVIN HOSKINSON

Ray Bradbury's Cold War Novels

In a discussion about the thematic content of *The Martian Chronicles* with interviewer David Mogen in 1980, Ray Bradbury stated, *"The Martian Chronicles* and *Fahrenheit 451* come from the same period in my life, when I was warning people. I was *preventing* futures." In this paring of the two books, Bradbury suggests a deep kinship between the pieces and indicates the probability that they are more than just successive novels in his overall body of work. Though the two fictions are usually read as separate entities, if read as complementary works, they provide a more comprehensive view of a larger whole. As consecutive arrivals in Bradbury's postwar publications, and in their mutual attraction to similar major themes of the cold war era, *The Martian Chronicles* and *Fahrenheit 451* distinguish themselves as Bradbury's "cold war novels."

The two works are on the surface entirely different kinds of fiction. *The Martian Chronicles* is a collection of twenty-six chapters (most originally published as short stories), written between 1944 and 1950 and linked primarily by their setting on the planet Mars between the years 1999 and 2026. Since many of the stories were separately conceived, most of the characters in the finished book are contained within their individual tales and do not cross over into other chapters. And though Mars is in many ways the centerpiece of the book, and its treatment by the humans is "chronicled"

From *Extrapolation* 36, no. 4. © 1995 by The Kent State University Press. (Originally published as *"The Martian Chronicles* and *Fahrenheit 451:* Ray Bradbury's Cold War Novels.")

over a twenty-seven-year period, there is no "protagonist" in the pure sense of the term, nor is there a "plot" common to the separate sections. In contrast, *Fahrenheit 451* is structured as a novel, divided into three chapters; it is set on Earth; it is the story of one central protagonist, Guy Montag; and the plot of the novel—Montag's liberation from Captain Beatty and his acceptance of a new purpose in a new civilization—is carefully mapped out.

These surface differences of structure, character, and setting notwithstanding, *The Martian Chronicles* and *Fahrenheit 451* share a distinction as "cold war fiction" because in them, much more deliberately than in earlier or later publications, Bradbury deals with subjects and issues that were shaped by the political climate of the United States in the decade immediately following World War II. A number of significant events during these years transformed the character of America from a supremely confident, Nazi-demolishing world leader to a country with deep insecurities, one suddenly suspicious and vigilant of Communist activity within its citizenry. First, Joseph Stalin's immediate and unchecked occupation of Eastern European countries at the close of World War II left many Americans wondering if the United States and the Roosevelt administration hadn't foolishly misjudged Soviet intentions at the Yalta Conference in 1945. Second, the Soviet Union's subsequent acquisition of atomic weapons technology by 1949 would reinforce this position; it would also end the U.S. monopoly on thermonuclear weapons and raise questions about Communist agents in high-level government positions. Third, Senator Joseph McCarthy's public accusations of Communist activity in the State Department in 1950 (together with the inflammatory tactics of J. Edgar Hoover, the FBI, and a host of other right-wing government agencies) planted seeds of paranoia and subversion in the American culture that would blossom into fear and irrationality throughout the 1950s. As David Halberstam points out, "It was a mean time. The nation was ready for witch-hunts." Through his examination of government oppression of the individual, the hazards of an atomic age, recivilization of society, and the divided nature of the "Cold War Man," Ray Bradbury uses *The Martian Chronicles* and *Fahrenheit 451* to expose the "meanness" of the cold war years.

During the Truman years of the early cold war, when the administration attempted to reverse the image of the Democratic party as being "soft" on communism, the U.S. government attempted to silence individuals who were thought to be "potentially disloyal" through various offices such as the Justice Department and the Loyalty Review Board. ⟨Historian Alan Theoharis notes that⟩ Truman himself released a press statement in July 1950 that granted authority over national security matters to the FBI. The statement expressed grave concern over "the Godless Communist Cause" and further warned that "it is important to learn to know the enemies of the American way of life." For Bradbury, such government-supported conformism amounted to censorship and ultimately led to the fostering of what William F. Touponce labels "mass culture" and what Kingsley Amis calls "conformist hell." We see Bradbury's strong distrust of "majority-held" views and official doctrine positions in several places in *The Martian Chronicles*; these areas of distrust, moreover, recur in *Fahrenheit 451*.

In the seventh chapter of *Chronicles*, "—And the Moon Be Still as Bright" (originally published in 1948), the fierceness of the individual and the official will of the majority clash violently in the persons of Jeff Spender and Captain Wilder. Spender is a crewman on the Fourth Expedition to Mars who feels a sense of moral outrage at the behavior of his fellow crewmen upon landing. While Biggs, Parkhill, and others break out the liquor and throw a party upon their successful mission, Spender is revolted at their dancing and their harmonica playing on the Martian landscape and at Biggs's throwing of wine bottles into canals and vomiting on the tiled city floors. Spender marvels at Martian literature and ancient art forms, and he views the others' actions as sacrilegious, lamenting that "We Earth Men have a talent for ruining big, beautiful things." Like Spender, Captain Wilder also perceives the beauty of the cities; but as the officer of the crew, he does not allow his sympathies with Spender to override his need as commander in chief to preserve authoritative control of the mission. He doles out a perfunctory fifty-dollar fine to Spender for punching Biggs and orders Spender to "go back [to the party] and play happy"; later, following Spender's desertion and mutinous killing of several crewmen, Wilder acknowledges that he has "too much earth blood" to accept Spender's invitation to stay on Mars without the others. Wilder is convinced by this time that he must stop Spender, but he is tormented by an uncertainty over whether he is stopping him because he believes Spender is wrong or whether he simply lacks Spender's individual conviction to lash out against the will of the majority: "I hate this feeling of thinking I'm doing right when I'm not really certain I am. Who are we, anyway? The majority? Is that the answer? . . . What is this majority and who are in it? And what do they think and how did they get that way and will they ever change and how the devil did I get caught in this rotten majority? I don't feel comfortable." In order to preclude the disintegration of the mission, Wilder shoots Spender before Spender can kill anyone else. But the issue of individuality vs. conformity that has been raised by Spender's mutiny has not been resolved for the captain. The next day, Wilder knocks out Parkhill's teeth after Parkhill has shot out the windows of some of the buildings in a dead city. Wilder here releases his inner rage at his own ambivalent compliance with a "government finger point[ing] from four-color posters" described in the book's next chapter, "The Settlers." On the one hand, he has eliminated the disruptive presence of an outlaw; on the other hand, in so doing he has taken the Official Position and removed from the expedition the value of "the most renegade of Bradbury's frontiersmen" as well as the one other individual who valued art and creative expression.

Bradbury picks up this theme of distrust for the officially endorsed view again in "Usher II," the seventeenth chapter of *Chronicles* (originally published in 1950 prior to the publication of the full book). In this chapter William Stendahl designs a replica of Edgar Allan Poe's House of Usher on Mars. His intent is twofold: to pay tribute to Poe and "to teach [the Clean-Minded people] a fine lesson for what [they] did to Mr. Poe on Earth," which was to burn his works (along with the works of others who wrote "tales of the future") in the Great Fire of 1975. Here again Bradbury rejects the will of the majority through Stendahl's speech to Bigelow, the architect of Usher II. Stendahl sermonizes to Bigelow that the Great Fire came about because "there was always a minority afraid of something, and a great majority afraid of the dark, afraid of the future, afraid of the past, afraid of the present, afraid of themselves and shadows of themselves." Another neurosis Bradbury places in Stendahl's litany of fears has roots in the "red scare" policies enacted through McCarthyist tactics in 1950s America: "Afraid of the word 'politics' (which eventually became a synonym for Communism among the more reactionary elements, so I hear, and it was worth your life to use the word!) . . ." Later, at the party Stendahl throws for his invited guests, the Moral Climates people, Stendahl kills all the "majority guests" with different approaches to murders seen in Poe's stories. At the end of the chapter, Stendahl mortars up Moral Climates Investigator Garrett into a brick wall because Garrett "took other people's advice that [Poe's books] needed burning." In contrast with "—And the Moon Be Still as Bright," where the individual is martyred by the majority, the individual in "Usher II" enjoys a sinister triumph over the majority.

In *Fahrenheit 451* Bradbury resumes his attack on government-based censorship encountered earlier in "Usher II." Set on Earth rather than on Mars, this novel follows the metamorphosis of Guy Montag, a fireman (a starter of fires in this future dystopian society) who comes to question and break free of the government that employs him to burn books. The novel opens with Montag having just returned to the firehouse after igniting another residence, "grinn[ing] the fierce grin of all men singed and driven back by flame." He is clearly of the majority at this point, loyal to his job and proud of wearing the salamander and the phoenix disc, the official insignia of the Firemen of America. But seventeen-year-old Clarisse McClellan, who is dangerous in Beatty's eyes because "she [doesn't] want to know *how* a thing [is] done, but *why*," points out some disturbing facts that Montag cannot escape: he answers her questions quickly without thinking; he can't remember if he knew there was dew on early-morning grass or not; he can't answer the question of whether he is happy or not. A growing unrest with his own lack of individual sensibilities creeps into Montag at Clarisse's challenges. As Donald Watt observes, Clarisse is "catalytic" and "dominant in Montag's growth to awareness"; her role for Montag parallels the role of Spender for Captain Wilder, planting the seed of doubt that enacts a process of critical self-examination. These doubts about the government he is serving accumulate through the latest suicide attempt by Montag's wife, Mildred (and her casual acceptance of this attempt after she is resuscitated); through his witnessing of a book-hoarding woman who chose to ignite her own home rather than flee in the face of the firemen's flamethrowers; through the government's systematic elimination of Clarisse; through his own growing need to read and understand books.

Montag ultimately realizes that he cannot return to the firehouse. At this point he rejects both the realm of the majority and his association with Chief Beatty, who professes to "stand against the small tide of those who want to make everyone unhappy with conflicting theory and thought." Montag's liberation from the Firemen of America is augmented when he locates Faber (a former English professor and current member of the book-preserving underground), who offers Montag moral counsel and employs him as an infiltrator at the firehouse. Mildred, in the meantime, breaks her silence and sounds a fire alarm at the Montag residence. In a dramatic confrontation of Individual vs. State, Montag refuses Beatty's orders to burn his own house and instead turns the flamethrower on Beatty. This revolt severs Montag from the majority permanently; he then joins the underground movement to preserve books for the future as global war descends on the city.

Another theme of the cold war years Bradbury takes up in both novels is the precariousness of human existence in an atomic age. The eventual "success" of the Manhattan Project in 1945, which resulted in the development of the atomic bomb, came about only after several years' worth of blind groping toward the right physics equations by some of the brightest physicists in the world. The scientists were literally guessing about how to detonate the bomb, how big to make the bomb, and, most significantly, how strong the bomb would be. The project itself, in the words of Lansing Lamont, was "a bit like trying to manufacture a new automobile with no opportunity to test the engine beforehand." After studying various reports on a wide range of explosions in known history, the Los Alamos physicists determined that the atom bomb's force would fall somewhere in between the volcanic eruption of Krakatau in 1883 (which killed 36,000 people and was heard 3,000 miles away) and the 1917 explosion of the munitions ship *Mont Blanc* in Halifax Harbor, Nova Scotia (killing 1,100)—"hopefully a lot closer to Halifax," Lamont notes, "but just where [the scientists] couldn't be sure." The subsequent explosions at Hiroshima and Nagasaki made Americans more "sure" of the bomb's potential but not sure at all about whether the knowledge of its potential was worth the price of having created it in the first place. As a line of military defense against the spread of nazism, the bomb became a prime example of how science unleashed can, according to Gary Wolfe, produce "the alienation of humanity from the very technological environments it has constructed in order to resolve its alienation from the universe."

It is difficult to comprehend the depth to which the atom bomb terrified the world, and America specifically, in the early cold war era. Richard Rhodes, author of *The Making of the Atomic Bomb*, writes that "A nuclear weapon is in fact a total-death machine, compact and efficient" and quotes a Japanese study that concludes that the explosions at Hiroshima and Nagasaki were "the opening chapter to the annihilation of mankind." More than any single technological development, the atomic bomb made people think seriously about the end of the world. As a passport to Wolfe's icon of the wasteland, the bomb "teaches us that the unknown always remains, ready to reassert itself, to send us back to the beginning."

Bradbury first captures the general sense of anxiety felt in a new atomic age in the fifth chapter of *The Martian Chronicles*, "The Taxpayer." This short chapter identifies fear of nuclear war as an impetus for leaving Earth; the chapter also establishes itself as one of several in *Chronicles* that serve as precursors to *Fahrenheit 451* and centralize many of the early cold war themes Bradbury resumes in the second book: "There was going to be a big atomic war on Earth in about two years, and he didn't want to be here when it happened. He and thousands of others like him, if they had any sense, would go to Mars. See if they wouldn't! To get away from wars and censorship and statism and conscription and government control of this and that, of art and science!"

Once the fear-of-nuclear-holocaust theme is introduced in the book, Bradbury structures the story-chapters so that references to the bomb and to atomic war in *Chronicles* are periodically repeated, thus sustaining anxiety throughout the novel. One of Jeff Spender's fears in "—And the Moon Be Still as Bright," for example, is that war on Earth will lead to "atomic research and atom bomb depots on Mars"; he is willing to kill off the members of the Fourth Expedition in order to keep Earth from "flopping their filthy atom bombs up here, fighting for bases to have wars." "The Luggage Store," a later bridge chapter that echoes the points made in "The Taxpayer," picks up the theme of atomic war on Earth in the year 2005. In discussing whether or not members of the Earth society transplanted on Mars will return to Earth when the war begins, Father Peregrine explains to the proprietor of the luggage store man's inability to comprehend atomic war from millions of miles away: "[Earth is] so far away it's unbelievable. It's not here. You can't touch it. You can't even see it. All you see is a green light. Two billion people living on that light? Unbelievable! War? We don't hear the explosions." The expanse of the physical distance between Earth and Mars in his dialogue mirrors the uneasy diplomatic distance the United States and the Soviet Union managed to somehow sustain throughout the cold war years, which kept atomic war in the abstract then as well.

In November 2005, however, the Mars inhabitants receive a light-radio message in "The Watchers": "AUSTRALIAN CONTINENT ATOMIZED IN PREMATURE EXPLOSION OF ATOMIC STOCKPILE. LOS ANGELES, LONDON BOMBED. WAR." The resulting picture of Mars—and Earth—for the remaining forty-two pages of the novel is desolate and, for the most part, apocalyptic. Viewers on Mars could point a telescope at Earth and see New York explode, or London "covered with a new kind of fog." Bradbury also employs humor in driving home the gravity of nuclear catastrophe. In one of the novel's more ironic and darkly humorous chapters, "The Silent Towns," Walter Gripp believes himself the only man left on Mars following the wartime emigration back to Earth by most of the planet's inhabitants. Never having found "a quiet and intelligent woman" to marry when Mars was fully inhabited, Walter is shocked by the sound of a ringing phone. On the other end is the voice of Genevieve Selsor. Ecstatic, he arranges to meet her and conjures up a beautiful woman with "long dark hair shaking in the wind" and "lips like red peppermints." When he meets her and sees that she in fact has a "round and thick" face with eyes "like two immense eggs stuck into a white mess of bread dough," he endures a painful evening with her before fleeing for a life of solitary survivalism. Though the chapter provides a moment of levity compared to the ruined civilization chapters that follow and close out the book, the humor in "The Silent Towns" is carefully crafted toward nervousness. It is in the vein of comedy Donald Hassler identifies in *Comic Tones in Science Fiction: The Art of Compromise with Nature* that "refuse[s] to be tragic and yet [is] filled with pathos because [it] represents *just* survival." The story's humor serves primarily to deromanticize the last-man-on-earth motif: though atomic war may have made Walter Gripp a master of all he surveys, it has also perpetuated and intensified his isolation.

"There Will Come Soft Rains," the novel's penultimate chapter, restores the tone in *The Martian Chronicles* to grimness, depicting the "tomb planet" character of Mars alluded to one chapter earlier in "The Long Years." The "character" in this chapter is an ultramodern home on post–atomic war Earth in 2026, equipped with turn-of-the-twenty-first-century gadgetry. A voice-clock repeats the time of day each minute, and a kitchen ceiling reads off the date. The automatic kitchen cooks breakfast for four; the patio walls open up into bridge tables; the nursery walls glow and animate themselves at children's hour; the beds warm their own sheets; and the tub fills itself with bath water. This technology wastes away mindlessly, however, for "the gods had gone away." This is the wasteland of thermonuclear destruction: the home is "the one house left standing" in a "ruined city" whose "radioactive glow could be seen for miles." The only signs of life (other than the various "small cleaning animals, all rubber and metal") are a dying dog and the evidence of a family vaporized by atomic explosion: "The entire west face of the house was black, save for five places. Here the silhouette in paint of a man mowing a lawn. Here, as in a photograph, a woman bent to pick flowers. Still farther over, their images burned on wood in one titanic instant, a small boy, hands flung into the air; higher up, the image of a thrown ball, and opposite him, a girl, hands raised to catch a ball which never came down." The chapter ends with the house endlessly spinning out its daily mechanical routine to the ghosts of its vaporized inhabitants. It is perhaps the most vivid image Bradbury's cold war novels offer of the synthetic hell man makes for himself from the raw materials of science, technology, and irrationality.

Fahrenheit 451 resumes the examination of precarious existence in an atomic age that Bradbury began in *The Martian Chronicles*. Fire as the omnipotent weapon in *Fahrenheit* finds metaphoric parallels in the notion of the bomb as the omnipotent force in the cold war years. The early tests of the Los Alamos project, for example, paid close attention to the extreme temperatures produced by the fissioning and fusioning of critical elements. J. Robert Oppenheimer, Niels Bohr, and Edward Teller based key decisions in the atomic bomb (and later the hydrogen bomb) designs on the core temperatures created at the moment of detonation. Montag and the Firemen of America, likewise, are ever conscious of the key numeral 451 (the temperature at which books burn), so much so that it is printed on their helmets. The linking of hubris with the attainment of power is evident in both the Los Alamos scientists and the Firemen as well. As the Manhattan Project was drawing to a close, the team of physicists who designed the bomb came to exude a high degree of pride in their mastery of science, but without an attendant sense of responsibility. As Lamont explains, the bomb "represented the climax of an intriguing intellectual match between the scientists and the cosmos. The prospect of solving the bomb's cosmic mysteries, of having their calculations proved correct, seemed far more fascinating and important to the scientists than the prospect of their opening an era obsessed by fear and devoted to the control of those very mysteries." *Fahrenheit 451* opens with Montag similarly blinded by his own perceived importance: "He knew that when he returned to the firehouse, he might wink at himself, a minstrel man, burnt-corked, in the mirror. Later, going to sleep, he would feel the fiery smile still gripped by his face muscles, in the dark. It never went away, that smile, it never ever went away, as long as he remembered." Like the engineers of atomic destruction, the engineer of intellectual destruction feels the successful completion of his goals entitles him to a legitimate smugness. The work of the cold war physicists, in retrospect, also shares something else with Montag, which Donald Watt points out: "Montag's destructive burning . . . is blackening, not enlightening; and it poses a threat to nature."

Fahrenheit 451 also expands on the anxiety over the atomic bomb and fear of a nuclear apocalypse introduced in *Chronicles*. In *Fahrenheit*, Beatty endorses the official government position that, as "custodians of our peace of mind," he and Montag should "let [man] forget there is such a thing as war." Once Montag has decided to turn his back on the firehouse, however, he tries conveying his personal sense of outrage to Mildred at being kept ignorant, hoping to incite a similar concern in her: "How in hell did those bombers get up there every single second of our lives! Why doesn't someone want to talk about it! We've started and won two atomic wars since 1990!" Mildred, however, is perfectly uninspired and breaks off the conversation to wait for the White Clown to enter the TV screen. But Montag's unheeded warning becomes reality; the bombs are dropped once Montag meets up with Granger and the book people, just as they became reality in "There Will Come Soft Rains," and Montag's horrific vision of the bomb's shock wave hitting the building where he imagines Mildred is staying captures a chilling image of his ignorant wife's last instant of life:

> Montag, falling flat, going down, saw or felt, or imagined he saw
> or felt the walls go dark in Millie's face, heard her screaming,
> because in the millionth part of time left, she saw her own face
> reflected there, in a mirror instead of a crystal ball, and it was
> such a wild empty face, all by itself in the room, touching
> nothing, starved and eating of itself, that at last she recognized it
> as her own and looked quickly up at the ceiling as it and the
> entire structure of the hotel blasted down upon her, carrying her
> with a million pounds of brick, metal, plaster, and wood, to meet

other people in the hives below, all on their quick way down to
the cellar where the explosion rid itself of them in its own unrea-
sonable way.

Perhaps Bradbury's own sense of fear at a future that must accommodate
atomic weapons had intensified between *The Martian Chronicles*'s publication in 1950 and *Fahrenheit 451*'s completion in 1953; perhaps what David
Mogen identifies as Bradbury's inspiration for the book, Hitler's book
burnings, affords little room for the comic. For whatever reasons, unlike
Chronicles, which intersperses the solemnity of its nuclear aftermath chapters with a bit of lightness in the Walter Gripp story, *Fahrenheit* sustains a
serious tone to the end of the book, even in its resurrectionist optimism for
the future of the arts.

   This optimism for the future—this notion of recivilization—is the
third common element between *The Martian Chronicles* and *Fahrenheit 451*
that has early cold war connections. Given such nihilistic phenomena of the
cold war era as its tendencies toward censorship, its socially paranoid
outlook, and its budding arms race, it may seem a strange period to give rise
to any optimism. However, one of the great ironies of the period was a
peripheral belief that somehow the presence of nuclear arms would, by their
very capacity to bring about ultimate destruction to all humans, engender a
very special sort of cautiousness and cooperative spirit in the world hereto-
fore not experienced. Perhaps there was a belief that Hiroshima and
Nagasaki had taught us a big enough lesson in themselves about nuclear cataclysm that we as humans would rise above our destructive tendencies and live
more harmoniously. One very prominent figure who espoused this position
was Dr. J. Robert Oppenheimer, the very man who headed the Los Alamos
Manhattan Project. Oppenheimer would emerge as one of the most morally
intriguing characters of the cold war. He was among the first in the scientific
community to encourage restraint, caution, and careful deliberation in all
matters regarding the pursuit of atomic energy. "There is only one future of
atomic explosives that I can regard with any enthusiasm: that they should
never be used in war," he said in a 1946 address before the George Westing-
house Centennial Forum. He also refused to participate in the development
of the hydrogen bomb following Los Alamos, calling such a weapon "the
plague of Thebes" (Rhodes). In one of his most inspired addresses on the
cooperation of art and science, Oppenheimer stated that "Both the man of
science and the man of art live always at the edge of mystery, surrounded by
it; both always, as the measure of their creation, have had to do with the
harmonization of what is new with what is familiar, with the balance between
novelty and synthesis, with the struggle to make partial order in total chaos.

They can, in their work and in their lives, help themselves, help one another, and help all men."

Such a spirit of hope for renewed goodwill among men of all vocations is the optimistic vein through which society is reenvisioned following the atomic devastation of the Earth in "The Million-Year Picnic," the final chapter of *The Martian Chronicles*. Several days in the past, a rocket that had been hidden on Earth during the Great War carried William and Alice Thomas and their children, Timothy, Michael, and Robert, to Mars, presumably for a "picnic." The father admits to his inquisitive sons on this day, however, that the picnic was a front for an escape from life on Earth, where "people get lost in a mechanical wilderness" and "Wars got bigger and bigger and finally killed Earth." The father literally plans a new civilization: he blows up their rocket to avoid discovery by hostile Earthmen; he burns up all the family's printed records of their life on earth; and he now awaits, with his family, "a handful of others who'll land in a few days. Enough to start over. Enough to turn away from all that back on Earth and strike out on a new line." When his son Michael repeats his request to see a "Martian," the father takes his family to the canal and points to their reflections in the water. The book's last line, "The Martians stared back up at them for a long, long silent time from the rippling water," is optimistic without being didactic. It suggests that this new society has in fact already begun, that it is already "making partial order out of total chaos," as Oppenheimer suggests the cold war future needs to do. William F. Touponce believes that it is "an altogether appropriate ending" that "summarizes the experience of the reader, who has seen old illusions and values destroyed only to be replaced with new and vital ones." It also offers an image that invites the reader to extrapolate on the father's vision of "a new line" and trust the will of the colonizers for once.

Bradbury's optimism for a recivilized world is also evident in the conclusion of *Fahrenheit 451*. The seed for an optimistic ending to this dystopian work is actually planted just before the bombs strike. As Montag makes his way across the wilderness, dodging the pursuit of the mechanical hound and the helicopters, he spots the campfire of the book people. His thoughts reflect an epiphany of his transformation from a destroyer of civilization to a builder of it: "[The fire] was not burning. It was *warming*. He saw many hands held to its warmth, hands without arms, hidden in darkness. Above the hands, motionless faces that were only moved and tossed and flickered with firelight. He hadn't known fire could look this way. He had never thought in his life that it could give as well as take." This spirit of giving, of creating from the environment, is emphasized throughout the speeches given by Granger, the leader of the book preservers. In his allusion to the phoenix, which resurrects itself from the ashes of its own pyre,

Granger's words reflect the new Montag, who can now see the life-sustaining properties of fire as well as its destructive powers; hopefully, Granger's words also contain hope for the American response to Hiroshima and Nagasaki: "we've got one damn thing the phoenix never had. We know the damn silly thing we just did. We know all the damn silly things we've done for a thousand years and as long as we know that and always have it around where we can see it, someday we'll stop making the goddamn funeral pyres and jumping in the middle of them." The book ends with Montag rehearsing in his mind a passage from the Book of Revelation, which he says he'll save for the reading at noon. Peter Sisario sees in this ending "a key to Bradbury's hope that 'the healing of nations' can best come about through a rebirth of man's intellect"; Sisario's interpretation of *Fahrenheit*'s ending and Oppenheimer's interpretation of mankind's necessary response to the cold war share a belief in the triumph of the benevolent side of humans.

A fourth theme in Bradbury's cold war novels that has a historical "objective correlative" is the dichotomous nature of the Cold War Man. The Cold War Man is a man antagonized by conflicting allegiances—one to his government, the other to his personal sense of morals and values—who is forced by circumstance to make an ultimate choice between these impulses. This Bradbury character type has roots in cold war political tensions.

During the early cold war years, the United States's international stance frequently wavered between a policy of military supremacy and one of peacetime concessions. One historian notes this phenomenon in the about-face many Americans took toward Roosevelt's role in the shifting of global powers following World War II: " . . . both policy and attitude changed with the Truman administration. The rationale behind Yalta—that a negotiated agreement with the Soviet Union was possible and that the development of mutual trust was the best means to a just and lasting peace—was now rejected in favor of the containment policy and superior military strength" (Theoharis).

These contradictory stances of peace and aggression in our nation's outlook occasionally found expression in the form of a single man during the early cold war. The figure of Dr. J. Robert Oppenheimer again becomes relevant. Though primarily remembered for his contribution to physics, Oppenheimer also had strong leanings toward the humanities; as a youth and in his years as a Harvard undergraduate, he developed a range of literary interests from the Greek classicists to Donne to Omar Khayyam. David Halberstam observes, "To some he seemed the divided man—part creator of the most dangerous weapon in history—part the romantic innocent searching for some inner spiritual truth." For a government-employed physicist, however, this "division" would turn out to be something of a tragic flaw in the cold war years. When Oppenheimer would have no part of the U.S. government's decision to pursue the hydrogen bomb in its initial phase of the arms race with the Soviets, the government began an inquiry into his past. It was "determined" in June of 1954 that Oppenheimer was guilty of Communist associations that jeopardized national security. He was then stripped of his government security clearance, and his service with the Atomic Energy Commission terminated. Thus, in Oppenheimer was a man whose pacifistic sympathies eventually triumphed over his capacity for aggression—and in the early cold war years he was punished for it.

The Oppenheimer figure finds interesting parallels in Bradbury's cold war novels. In "—And the Moon Be Still as Bright" in *The Martian Chronicles*, Spender is torn between the need to serve his Earth-based government (in his participation with the expedition crew on Mars) and the deep personal need to preserve the remains of the native Martian culture, which he believes is threatened by the very kind of expedition he is serving: "When I got up here I felt I was not only free of [Earth's] so-called culture, I felt I was free of their ethics and their customs. I'm out of their frame of reference, I thought. All I have to do is *kill you all off* and *live my own life*" (emphasis added). Spender's surrender to the personal impulse to defend Mars from Earth corruption over the impulse to follow the government-entrusted group leads to his death. Wilder is forced to shoot Spender when he threatens more killings, and his death-image symbolically reinforces his divided self: "Spender lay there, his hands clasped, one around the gun, the other around the silver book that glittered in the sun." The gun, which is entrusted to him as a member of the expedition and the book, which he found in his walks through the Martian ruins, emblematize Spender's divided allegiances. The image is curiously akin to the image Lansing Lamont provides of Oppenheimer's dichotomous self: "With balanced equanimity he could minister to a turtle and select the target cities for the first atomic massacres." Wilder also exudes characteristics of the dichotomous Cold War Man. The captain's sympathies toward the arts and toward Spender's appreciation of them lead him to bury Spender with an aesthetic touch. Finding a Martian sarcophagus, Wilder has the crew "put Spender into a silver case with waxes and wines which were ten thousand years old, his hands folded on his chest." The scene immediately changes from Spender's ornate sarcophagus to the captain's catching Parkhill in one of the dead cities and knocking his teeth out for shooting at the Martian towers. Wilder's coexistent propensity for violence and aesthetic sensibilities mark his dichotomous cold war sides as well. Stendahl in "Usher II" further reflects both sides of this Cold War Man. He possesses the aesthetic appreciation of a literature devotee, a man with an architectural vision of Usher II, specifying to Bigelow the need for colors precisely "desolate and terrible," for walls that are "bleak," for tarn that is "black and lurid," for sedge that is "gray and ebon." Yet this same man furnishes his home with all of Poe's macabre instruments of death: an ape that strangles humans, a razor-sharp pendulum, a coffin for the nailing up of a live woman, and bricks and mortar for sealing up a live victim.

The dichotomous Cold War Man theme is again treated in *Fahrenheit 451*. Both Montag and Beatty are simultaneously capable of the destructive and appreciative of the artistic. As Donald Watt remarks of Montag, "Burning as constructive energy, and burning as apocalyptic catastrophe, are the symbolic poles of Bradbury's novel." Montag's divided self is clearly displayed by Bradbury at moments when his character is being influenced by the intellectually stimulating presences of Clarisse and Faber. Early in the book, when Montag is just beginning to wrestle with his identity as a fireman, Clarisse tells him that being a fireman "just doesn't seem right for you, somehow." Immediately Bradbury tells us that Montag "felt his body divide itself into a hotness and a coldness, a softness and a hardness, a trembling and a not trembling, the two halves grinding one upon the other." Later, after offering his services to Faber and his group, Montag considers the shiftings of his own character that he has been feeling in his conflicting allegiances: "Now he knew that he was two people, that he was, above all, Montag, who knew nothing, who did not even know himself a fool, but only suspected it. And he knew that he was also the old man who talked to him and talked to him as the train was sucked from one end of the night city to the other." Fire Chief Beatty also suggests aspects of the Cold War Man. In spite of his wearing the role of the Official State Majority Leader as the fire chief and relentlessly burning every book at every alarm, Beatty acknowledges that he knows the history of Nicholas Ridley, the man burned at the stake alluded to by the woman who ignites her own home. He gives Montag the reply that most fire captains are "full of bits and pieces"; however, when he later warns Montag against succumbing to the "itch" to read that every fireman gets "at least once in his career," he further adds an ambiguous disclosure: "Oh, to *scratch* that itch, eh? Well, Montag, take my word for it, I've had to read a few in my time to know what I was about, and the books say *nothing*! Nothing you can teach or believe." Though Beatty has an alibi for having some knowledge of literature, Bradbury urges us to question just what Beatty may *not* be telling us. Montag's later certainty over Beatty's desire to die at Montag's hands raises even more questions about Beatty's commitment to the destructive half of his duality.

Through *The Martian Chronicles* and *Fahrenheit 451*, Ray Bradbury has created a microcosm of early cold war tensions. Though the reader will perceive a degree of Bradbury's sociopolitical concerns from a reading of either novel, it is only through the reading of both as companion pieces that his full cold war vision emerges. From the perspective that America has wrestled itself free of the extremism of the McCarthyists and, thus far, has escaped nuclear war as well, Bradbury's cold war novels may have indeed contributed to the "prevention" of futures with cold war trappings.

RAFEEQ O. McGIVERON

The Imagery of Hands in Fahrenheit 451

Ray Bradbury's 1953 *Fahrenheit 451* contains a number of interesting stylistic devices. Robert Reilly praises Bradbury for having a style "like a great organ. . . ." David Mogen comments on the novel's "vivid style." Peter Sisario applauds the "subtle depth" of Bradbury's allusions, and Donald Watt pursues Bradbury's bipolar "symbolic fire" imagery. In recent articles I discussed Bradbury's use of mirror imagery and nature imagery.

In addition, throughout *Fahrenheit 451* Bradbury uses imagery of hands, making them significant reflectors of conscience. The hands of the misguided are deceptively calm, reflecting the complacency of self-righteousness. At the same time, the hands of the character struggling for right seem to do good almost of their own volition, even before the mind has been consciously decided. Finally, once characters are committed to positive action, their hands become an unambiguous force for good.

As the novel opens, "fireman" Guy Montag joyously goes about his job of burning down a house found to contain books, and Bradbury describes Montag's hands with ironic majesty. According to Bradbury, "his hands were the hands of some amazing conductor playing all the symphonies of blazing and burning to bring down the tatters and charcoal ruins of history." This early in the story Montag does not yet recognize the true destruction of his profession; indeed, he finds it "a pleasure to burn." Montag's conscience is

From *The Explicator* 54, no. 3. © 1996 by Heldref Publications.

blithely clear—or perhaps pathetically blank—and his self-confident, self-aggrandizing hands are a reflection of this emptiness.

Montag, however, has from time to time been taking books from the forbidden libraries he burns. When we finally witness this, Montag's hands reflect the unacknowledged dictates of conscience:

> Montag's hand closed like a mouth, crushed the book with wild devotion, with an insanity of mindlessness to his chest.
> Montag had done nothing. His hand had done it all, his hand with a brain of its own, with a conscience and a curiosity in each trembling finger, had turned thief. Now it plunged the book back under his arm, pressed it tight to sweating armpit, rushed out empty . . .
> He gazed, shaken, at that white hand.

His hand, of course, is not possessed by "an insanity of mindlessness." On the contrary, Montag has "a conscience and a curiosity . . ." but, still unwilling to recognize them, he projects them into his hands.

Soon Montag visits Faber, a former literature professor, to try to enlist the old man's help. When Faber initially refuses, Montag holds out a Bible and "lets" his hands shock Faber into action:

> Montag stood there and waited for the next thing to happen. His hands, by themselves, like two men working together, began to rip the pages from the book. The hands tore the flyleaf and then the first and then the second page.
> Montag . . . let his hands continue.

Again Montag's hands express what his consciousness scarcely can recognize. He has no real wish to damage the old Bible, but his conscience apparently understands that Faber's help is even more important.

Once Montag returns to the firehouse, his hands feel restless under the gaze of Fire Captain Beatty, his superior:

> In Beatty's sight, Montag felt the guilt of his hands. His fingers were like ferrets that had done some evil. . . . [T]hese were the hands that had acted on their own, no part of him, here was where the conscience first manifested itself to snatch books. . . .

Though Montag still has trouble accepting responsibility for breaking away from the thoughtless destruction which had been his way of life, Bradbury significantly uses the word conscience again. Just as his hands first manifested his new conscience, now they reflect his nervousness at possible discovery.

Captain Beatty leads the quivering Montag through a series of literary allusions, yet while Montag's hands reflect his precarious mental position, when the mocking Beatty reaches out to check Montag's guiltily racing pulse, his "graceful fingers" reflect a dogged self-righteousness. Bradbury employs such ironic imagery to show that Beatty is still able to possess the kind of clear (or blank) conscience which the nervous Montag fortunately no longer has. Beatty unwittingly may be the novel's best spokesperson against the stifling anti-intellectualism of his society, but he refuses to let any doubts interfere with his work; unlike Montag's, his hands never waver.

Bare minutes after the tense firehouse scene, Beatty forces Montag to burn down his own house. As Beatty berates him and threatens to track down Faber, Montag finds himself "twitch[ing] the safety catch on the flame thrower." Again, Bradbury has the conscience drive the hands onward even before the conscious mind has reasoned out the situation: "Montag . . . himself glanced to his hands to see what new thing they had done. Thinking back later he could never decide whether the hands or Beatty's reaction to the hands gave him the final push toward murder."

Even when Montag finally kills the taunting Beatty, Bradbury displaces him syntactically from the center of the action. Describing Beatty, Bradbury writes, "And then he was a shrieking blaze, a jumping, sprawling, gibbering mannikin, no longer human or known, all writhing flame on the lawn as Montag shot one continuous pulse of liquid fire on him." While Bradbury does identify the actor as Montag rather than as his disembodied hands, the abrupt transformation of Beatty and the placement of Montag toward the end of the sentence emphasize the spontaneity of the action. Should any doubts remain about the correctness of the action of Montag's conscience-driven hands, Bradbury has Montag think moments later in his flight, "Beatty wanted to die." Though Montag would not have killed Beatty willingly, his hands expressed what he consciously understands only later: "[B]urn them or they'll burn you. . . . Right now it's as simple as that."

When Montag escapes into the wilderness and joins a group of book-memorizing intellectuals, his first glimpse of them shows only "many hands held to [the campfire's] warmth, hands without arms. . . ." After several pages of highly didactic conversation with the group's leader, Montag helps put out the campfire: "The men helped, and Montag helped, and there, in the wilderness, the men all moved their hands, putting out the fire together." Certainly putting out the fire is symbolic of stopping society's book burning, but Bradbury's explicit mention of hands seems equally symbolic, for now hands are revealed as an unambiguous force for good.

Montag shows this again when he realizes that the future will "come out our hands and our mouths." Good thus comes not only from thinking and talking but from actually doing as well. Bradbury reiterates this important point when Montag thinks, "I'll hold onto the world tight someday"; just as hands may carry out deeds of conscience before the mind has fully decided, once the decision has been made, the conscience-driven hands must then follow through.

With his imagery of hands, Bradbury seems to suggest that actions may indeed speak louder than words. It is doubtful that our hands will ever simply reflect the conscience as Montag's so conveniently do, but it is equally doubtless that they should. Though blind self-righteousness may be most comfortable, Bradbury shows that the uncertainty of following one's conscience is morally preferable.

RAFEEQ O. McGIVERON

What "Carried the Trick"?: Mass Exploitation and the Decline of Thought in Ray Bradbury's Fahrenheit 451

There is an interesting dichotomy in Ray Bradbury's 1953 ⟨novel⟩ *Fahrenheit 451*, a noticeable gap between the message that the author and we the readers receive from the novel and the message that the text actually seems to support. While I realize that some see little use for such old-fashioned attention to the text itself, *Fahrenheit 451* is such an overtly didactic work that it almost invites such examination. Surely even the staunchest reader-response critic would agree that Bradbury is trying to sell the readers on ideas that he has put into his story. Yet there is a discrepancy between the ideas the author is selling—and readers are buying—and the ideas he has let the whole rest of the text support. I suggest this not necessarily to label it as a weakness but to show that the novel is thereby just a little bit richer and probably truer to life than many have supposed.

The discrepancy lies in the book's subtle treatment of the relationship between mass exploitation and the decline of thought. Fire Captain Beatty, the novel's chief book-burner, explains that "technology, mass exploitation, and minority pressure carried the trick" of supplanting independent thought with conformity and leading to censorship. Clearly Bradbury wants us to notice these three culprits in his fictional world and to beware of them in our own society as well. Often, however, readers have a tendency to miss the real textual centrality of mass exploitation, focusing

From *Extrapolation* 37, no. 3. © 1996 by Kent State University Press.

instead on the minority pressure that Bradbury makes so much more apparent.

Technology allows for the existence of mass culture in the novel, and minority pressure helps enforce conformity, but the mass exploitation of easy gratification is the fundamental threat to thought, for this exploitation begins earlier than minority pressure, requires the participation of a far greater majority of the population, and has a more direct effect on the decline of thought. In Bradbury's work controllers of mass communication and other producers of entertainment exploit the public's desire for easy gratification by disseminating only mindless escapism, which the exploited willingly consume to the exclusion of independent thought. People grow unwilling to give up their pleasures, even momentarily, by thinking deeply about anything, and they also become unwilling to violate the norms of society by expressing any original thought. Recognizing this role of mass exploitation in the decline of thought is important because the lesson applies both in *Fahrenheit 451* and in the real world as well.

Robert Reilly claims that the novel is "a frightening picture of how the products of science can destroy persons and human values," but this is an unfortunate simplification. Although it helps maintain the conformist mass culture of *Fahrenheit 451*, technology itself does not cause the decline of thought, for people still make the important decisions. Controllers of mass communication and other producers of entertainment decide which ideas they will censor and which they will disseminate, and the public decides what it will enjoy, what it will believe, and how it will act. Fire Captain Beatty contrasts the "pastepudding norm" of modern mass communication with books, which once "appealed to a few people, here, there, everywhere . . . [and] could afford to be different." He is unable, however, to support the idea that technology itself causes people to abandon independent thought in favor of simple conformity. Beatty claims, for example, that when zippers replace buttons "a man lacks just that much time to think while dressing at dawn," yet he avoids the obvious fact that the man is making the decision about what and when to think. Willis E. McNelly is correct when he writes that the novel "is not . . . about the technology of the future," and so is Marvin E. Mengeling, who finds that "Bradbury is no reactionary, antimachine 'nut.'"

Faber, the old, former literature professor, explains the primacy of human choice to Guy Montag, the unsettled "fireman" who no longer wants to burn books: "The same infinite detail and awareness [which books have] could be projected through the radios and televisors, but are not." According to Faber, "you can't argue with the four-wall televisor. Why? The televisor is 'real.' It is immediate; it has dimension. It tells you what to think and blasts it in. It *must* be right. It *seems* so right. It rushes you on so quickly to its own conclusions your mind hasn't the time to protest, 'What nonsense!'" Yet despite the fact that Faber, "with all [his] knowledge and skepticism, . . . [has] never been able to argue with a one-hundred piece symphony orchestra, full color, three dimensions, and being in and part of those incredible parlors," he still has a small television he can "blot out with the palm of [his] hand," and so do the book-memorizing intellectuals whom Montag later meets after his flight from the city. Clearly Bradbury is not simply attacking technology in general or even electronic mass communication in specific. Though technology can be used to brainwash people, Professor Faber and the other intellectuals show that people themselves are responsible for the condition of their own intellects.

Unlike technology, intolerant minority pressure that seeks to stifle ideas instead of arguing against them is a major cause of the decline of independent thought in *Fahrenheit 451*. Walter E. Meyers refers to this when he claims that "the danger to ideas and to their embodiment in books" comes from "a desire not to offend" and from "the unofficial sanctions of the appropriately named 'pressure groups.'" My teaching experience with the book suggests to me that this is a very common thing for readers to think. It is easy to see why, for the unity and explicitness of the passage dealing with minority pressure make that pressure the single most noticeable and memorable cause of the decline of thought in the novel.

Beatty explains to Montag that in the past intolerant pressure groups were influential in stifling free expression, fostering the conformity that eventually allowed the government to begin its own censoring:

> Bigger the population, the more minorities. Don't step on the toes of the dog lovers, cat lovers, doctors, lawyers, merchants, chiefs, Mormons, Baptists, Unitarians, second-generation Chinese, Swedes, Italians, Germans, Texans, Brooklynites, Irishmen, people from Oregon or Mexico. The people of this book, this play, this TV serial are not meant to represent any actual painters, cartographers, mechanics anywhere. The bigger your market, Montag, the less you handle controversy, remember that! All the minor minor minorities with their navels to be kept clean. Authors, full of evil thoughts, lock up your typewriters. They *did*. Magazines became a nice blend of vanilla tapioca. Books . . . were dishwater.

Beatty thus not only directly claims minority pressure as a cause of intellectual self-censorship and conformity but also emphasizes its pervasiveness with his rhetoric, listing fully twenty-one pressure groups organized by ethnicity, religion, geography, occupation, and even pet preference. He shows that from the major to, in the case of dog and cat lovers, the ridiculously "minor minor," each narrow pressure group pares down free expression of individuals' thoughts a little more.

Beatty's reiteration of the idea just over a page later is similar in purpose, although its rhetoric is slightly more restrained. He explains, "You must understand that our civilization is so vast that we can't have our minorities upset and stirred": "Colored people don't like *Little Black Sambo*. Burn it. White people don't feel good about *Uncle Tom's Cabin*. Burn it. Someone's written a book on tobacco and cancer of the lungs? The cigarette people are weeping? Burn the book. Serenity, Montag. Peace, Montag. Take your fight outside. Better yet, into the incinerator." The mesmerizing Beatty again shows how intolerance for opposing ideas helps lead to the stifling of individual expression, and hence of thought.

While it is not actually part of the novel itself, Bradbury's postscript "Coda"—which between 1979 and 1982 was called the Afterword—likewise emphasizes the dangers of minority pressure. Commenting on the text, Bradbury claims that "Fire-Captain Beatty . . . describes[s] how the books were burned first by minorities, each ripping a page or a paragraph from this book, then that, until the day came when the books were empty and the minds shut and the libraries closed forever." Here, in the author's own explanation of his work, he reminds readers that the pressure of intolerant minorities is the "first" and presumably most important cause leading to the decline of thought.

Bradbury also repeats Beatty's idea of the dangers of minority pressure in relation to the real world: "There is more than one way to burn a book. And the world is full of people running about with lit matches. Every minority, be it Baptist/Unitarian, Irish/Italian/Octagenarian/Zen Buddhist, Zionist/Seventh-day Adventist, Women's Lib/Republican, Mattachine/Four Square Gospel feels it has the will, the right, the duty to douse the kerosene, light the fuse." Like Beatty, he emphasizes the pervasiveness of the problem by defining the pressure groups with ridiculous improbability.

In addition to the evidence of the text itself and of Bradbury's coda, we are more likely to see the dangers of minority pressure in the novel because of the widespread perception that such dangers exist in our own society. In the 1950s readers might have thought of McCarthyism or perhaps the pious efforts to "clean up" comic books. Today adult readers are aware of various pressure groups' campaigns against sexually explicit music, the burning of the American flag, or sex and violence on television. Moreover, the current debate about political correctness also helps shape how we read Bradbury. Awareness of these controversies is certain to make us even more aware of Bradbury's treatment of minority pressure.

The threat of "mass culture" has been recognized by Peter Sisario, John Huntington, and David Mogen, and the idea, though not the term, has also been used by Donald Watt, Kingsley Amis, and Charles F. Hamblen. No one, however, has followed up with an investigation of the real importance of mass exploitation, especially in relation to Beatty's overemphasized scapegoat, minority pressure.

Despite the obvious role of intolerant minority pressure in the decline of thought, the text actually shows mass exploitation to be the more serious problem. Whereas Beatty's discussion of minority pressure is explicit and highly coherent, comprising mainly most of a paragraph over half a page long, his discussion of mass exploitation is less explicit and is diluted through eight pages. Yet Beatty himself cites mass exploitation as a problem that began even earlier, and both his exposition and the rest of the text show that mass exploitation requires the participation of a far greater majority of the population and replaces thought with conformity even more directly than does minority pressure.

Mass exploitation in the novel begins long before minority pressure, as soon as technology allows for the development of mass communication and mass culture. According to Beatty, the trends leading up to censorship "really got started around a thing called the Civil War," when modern technology, beginning with photography, enabled communication "to have *mass.*" Presumably this metaphorical use of "mass" refers to the greater amount of information carried; whereas earlier oral and printed communication still left much information to the imagination of the audience, photography and, later, moving pictures shifted this "mass" from the audience to the means of communication themselves. Rather than challenge audiences, controllers of communication chose to rely on "mass" to sell, thereby simplifying the ideas being transmitted: "'And because they had mass, they became simpler,' said Beatty. 'Once, books appealed to a few people, here, there, everywhere. They could afford to be different. The world was roomy. But then the world got full of eyes and elbows and mouths. Double, triple, quadruple population. Films and radios, magazines, books leveled down to a sort of pastepudding norm.'" Although technology makes this change possible, technology itself is not the cause, as Faber's understanding of technology's capacity for projecting "infinite detail and awareness" indicates. Minority pressure is also not responsible for this reduction of communication to the "pastepudding norm," for Beatty does not even bother to bring that last problem into the discussion for another three pages. The more important problem is the pre-existing mass exploitation of easy gratification.

The responsibility for the decline of thought this exploitation causes belongs to a great majority of the population. Because the damage of minority pressure is caused primarily by intolerant pressure groups and secondarily by the controllers of communication who follow their wishes, the public is far less responsible; people for the most part may be unaware that pressure groups influence what they watch, hear, and read. Mass exploitation is very much different, however, for it is the result of the public's active desire to avoid controversy and difficult thought in favor of easy gratification and, eventually, intellectual conformity. Beatty tells Montag that the pressure for censorship and the abandonment of thought at first "didn't come from the Government down," and this is especially true of mass exploitation. The disseminators of mindless escapism are to some extent to blame, and the consumers of this escapism are guilty as well.

Bradbury names the exploiters only once. According to Beatty, they are the "publishers, exploiters, broadcasters" who "whirl man's mind around about so fast . . . that the centrifuge flings off all unnecessary, time-wasting thought." Phrased another way, the exploiters are the controllers of mass communication who appeal solely to the public's desire for pleasure. Although Beatty does not say it, the exploiters are also those who design and market the dangerously powerful automobiles and drugs that the society consumes. They are those who encourage the acceptance of, as Granger, the leader of the book-memorizers, says, "dream[s] made or paid for in factories." Knowing that the public prefers easy gratification to difficult contemplation and evaluation, the exploiters "empty the theaters save for clowns and furnish the rooms with glass walls and pretty colors running up and down the walls like confetti or blood or sherry or sauterne." Beatty's imagery here, effective as always, mirrors the triviality, violence, and intoxication of the four-wall televisions. While Beatty explicitly identifies the exploiters only once, their effect on society is apparent throughout the novel.

Although the exploiters bear some responsibility for the decline of thought, the exploited are at least as guilty, for they are willingly exploited. Faber remembers that "the public stopped reading of its own accord" and that when the newspapers died out "no one *wanted* them back. No one missed them." Because he did not speak out when he could have, Faber even considers himself to be guilty as well. He explains to Montag that after half a century of the vigorous pursuit of easy gratification, the book-burning firemen are "hardly necessary to keep things in line. So few want to be rebels any more." According to Faber, who paraphrases very closely from Henrik Ibsen's 1882 *An Enemy of the People*, "the most dangerous enemy to truth and freedom" is neither technology nor minority intolerance but "the solid unmoving cattle of the majority." This important statement seems to refer to the public's acceptance of and even craving for mind-numbing mass exploitation and the comfort of its resulting intellectual conformity.

Beatty shows a similar understanding when he notes that the public, "knowing what it want[s], spin[s] happily." He explains the motivation to Montag: "Ask yourself, What do people want in this country, above all? People want to be happy, isn't that right? Haven't you heard it all your life? I want to be happy, people say. Well, aren't they? Don't we keep them moving, don't we give them fun? That's all we live for, isn't it? For pleasure, for titillation? And you must admit our culture provides plenty of these." Beatty thus blames—or, according to his view, credits—not only the exploiters but the willingly exploited.

According to Clarisse, the inquisitive seventeen year old who helps Montag learn to question and wonder, people no longer really think or talk about anything important: "No, not anything. They name a lot of cars or swimming pools mostly and say how swell. But they all say the same things and nobody says anything different from anyone else." The public is happy to think of pleasure and brand names and talk in clichés.

One of the most pathetic examples of the public's willingness to allow itself to be exploited is not its attraction to obviously seductive pleasures but its automatic acceptance of even the least attractive things that the televisions and radios present. People are so accustomed to enjoying mindless mass communication that they also enjoy the accompanying commercials. While riding on the subway, Montag sees people "tapping their feet to the rhythm of Denham's Dentifrice, Denham's Dandy Dental Detergent, Denham's Dentifrice Dentifrice Dentifrice, one two, one two three, one two, one two three . . . mouths . . . faintly twitching the words Dentifrice Dentifrice Dentifrice." The masses are unwilling to break with conformity and relinquish even this least attractive "pleasure" by thinking for themselves.

Mass exploitation hastens the decline of thought even more directly than does intolerant minority pressure, for while pressure groups may make people avoid controversy, easily gratifying entertainment actually provides a seductive alternative to any and all difficult thought. Beatty neatly sums up the philosophy embodied by the mass exploitation of easy gratification: "Life is immediate, the job counts, pleasure lies all about after work. Why learn anything save pressing buttons, pulling switches, fitting nuts and bolts?" While minority pressure comes from a comparative few members of the public, the impetus for this exploitation comes instead from an over-whelming majority. "Publishers, exploiters, broadcasters" sense the public's desire for relaxation and pleasure and exploit this for profit by producing only entertainment which is easily gratifying, and the willingly exploited enjoy their freedom from independent thought.

Four main kinds of this exploitation exist in the novel: the simplifica-tion of intellectual challenges, competitive diversions, drug use, and commodifed physicality. Referring to such pleasurable distractions, Beatty says, "So bring on your clubs and parties, your acrobats and magicians, your daredevils, motorcycle helicopters, your sex and heroin, more of everything to do with automatic reflex." Easy gratification is to be pursued to the exclusion of independent thought.

Although, as Bradbury says in the coda, books may have been "burned first by the minorities," works of art with the potential to be challenging were simplified even earlier. Beatty shows that this exploitation of easy gratification began "around a thing called the Civil War" and rapidly accelerated in the twentieth century with the increasing sophistication of mass communication technology, when "films and radios, magazines, books leveled down to a sort of pastepudding norm." Beatty explains that intellectually challenging works were made easier so that they would appeal to a larger audience: "Classics cut to fit fifteen-minute radio shows, then cut again to fill a two-minute book column, winding up at last as a ten- or twelve-line dictionary resume. . . . [M]any were those whose sole knowledge of *Hamlet* . . . was a one-page digest in a book that claimed: *now at last you can read all the classics; keep up with your neighbors.*" In this example the exploitation is two-fold in that publishers play both on the public's desires for shorter and easier readings and on desires to "keep up with [the] neighbors" as well.

After such exploitative cutting, books and magazines were watered down still farther so that by the time of the novel only "comics, the good old confessions, [and] trade journals" survive. Drama on television has been simplified to the level of the "Clara Dove five-minute romance" and pointless serials featuring a "gibbering pack of tree apes that [say] nothing, nothing, nothing and [say] it loud, loud, loud." Presumably films are similar. Radio is simply "an electronic ocean of sound, of music and talk and music and talk" that figuratively drowns the listener. In a more visceral metaphor, radio "vomit[s] . . . a great tonload of tin, copper, silver, chromium, and brass . . . pound[ing listeners] into submission." Most sinister of all, Bradbury describes the ubiquitous thimble-sized ear radios rather ominously as "hidden wasp[s]," "electronic bees," and "praying mantis[es]." The novel's equivalent of music videos on the "musical wall" are now "only color and all abstract," and even such musical art as previously existed in record-playing machines has been so drained of emotion and changed in form that the machines have gradually become merely "joke boxes." Moreover, Clarisse says that in what passes for modern museums, art is "*all* abstract," paintings refusing to "[say] things or even [show] people" and thereby risk making people think. The public wants easily gratifying entertainment, the exploiters help make the situation worse by producing only that which requires no original thought to enjoy, and thought is gradually abandoned.

Moreover, education is simplified as "school is shortened, discipline relaxed, philosophies, histories, languages dropped, English and spelling gradually neglected, finally almost completely ignored." Clarisse tells Montag that school now stifles thought rather than encouraging it: "An hour of TV class, an hour of basketball or running, another hour of transcription history or painting pictures, and more sports, but do you know, we never ask questions, or at least most don't; they just run the answers at you, bing, bing, bing, and us sitting there for four more hours of film teacher." To ensure that children do not grow up to ask what Beatty calls "embarrassing" questions, the government has "lowered the kindergarten age year after year until now [it is] almost snatching them from the cradle." Even to parents school is simply a place to "plunk" the children in nine days out of ten."

This reflects and reinforces the conformity already manifested in the public's acceptance of simplified entertainment, for children who are never taught to think about anything challenging are unlikely to want to be challenged by their entertainment or by anything else. According to Beatty, when "school turn[s] out more runners, jumpers, racers, tinkerers, grabbers, snatchers, fliers, and swimmers instead of examiners, critics, knowers, and imaginative creators, the word 'intellectual,' of course, [becomes] the swear word it deserve[s] to be." Thus the simplification of education reinforces the public's existing desire to avoid difficult thought, reteaching the lesson already taught by mass entertainment: thoughtless conformity is simple and pleasurable.

Just as the simplification of intellectual challenges helps stifle independent thought by catering to and encouraging intellectual apathy, so does an emphasis on competitive diversions. Beatty shows how an overemphasis on sports can take the place of thought: "More sports for everyone, group spirit, fun, and you don't have to think, eh? Organize and organize and superorganize super-super sports." Beatty is even more explicit about the mindlessness of contests: "Give the people contests they win by remembering the words to more popular songs or the names of state capitals or how much corn Iowa grew last year. Cram them full of noncombustible data, chock them so damned full of 'facts' they feel stuffed, but absolutely 'brilliant' with information. Then they'll feel they're thinking, they'll get a *sense* of motion without moving." Feeling stuffed with unimportant facts thus replaces actual thinking. Likewise, Faber reminds Montag that most people are satisfied if they can "dance faster than the White Clown, shout louder than 'Mr. Gimmick' and the parlor 'families.'" Both sports and contests emphasize a simple competitiveness leading away from individual thought.

A more dangerous type of thought-destroying mass exploitation is socially condoned drug use. Heroin is the most powerful drug in the novel, and Beatty's reference to it is casual enough to suggest that its use is not uncommon. Although the sleeping pills prevalent in the society could be used responsibly, the book shows only escapist overuse. When Montag's wife, Millie, overdoses, perhaps accidentally, by taking "thirty or forty" pills, the medical technicians who detoxify her and replace her blood tell Montag that the problem is common: "We get these cases nine or ten a night. Got so many, starting a few years ago, we had the special machines built." Millie also shows that alcohol abuse is still widespread, for when she wakes in the morning with a headache and no memory of the previous night, her first thought is that she has a hangover from "a wild party or something." Just as people flee difficult thought with simplified challenges and competitive diversions, they also occupy their time with mind-altering drugs that, presumably, are marketed without care for their dangerous effects.

The most common of the distracting drugs is nicotine, which Bradbury often presents the enemies of thought as using. Beatty smokes compulsively. Bradbury's conspicuous imagery of flame and smoke certainly reflects the destructive burning of Beatty's profession, but the act itself also reveals the nervous behavior of a mind mechanically avoiding thought: later Bradbury shows Beatty smoking automatically, lighting up habitually without any fanfare. The medical "handymen" who save Millie's life, "the men with the cigarettes in their straight-lined mouths," are able to stand "with the cigarette smoke curling around their noses and into their eyes without making them blink or squint." Millie's imbecilic friends are similar, for when Guy turns off the television walls the women sit nervously "lighting cigarettes, blowing smoke." Later Montag tells Granger that when he tries to remember his wife, one of the only things he can see is that "there's a cigarette in [her hands]." Montag smokes early on in the novel, but as he grows more thoughtful Bradbury simply lets this habit disappear. For the others, however, the ritual of smoking fills the time that might otherwise be used for thought and self-reflection.

The final type of mass exploitation speeding the decline of thought is commodified physicality, both actual and vicarious. People can "head for a Fun Park to bully people around, break windowpanes in the Window Smasher place or wreck cars in the Car Wrecker place with the big steel ball." Powerful "beetle cars" are designed, and probably marketed, for "driving a hundred miles an hour, at a clip where you can't think of anything else but the danger." Millie often drives "a hundred miles an hour across town . . . hearing only the scream of the car," and late at night she likes to "get it up around ninety-five and . . . feel wonderful" hitting rabbits and dogs out in the country. Children as young as twelve might go "playing 'chicken' and 'knock hubcaps'" or go "out for a long night of roaring five or six hundred miles in a few moonlit hours, their faces icy with wind, . . . coming home or not coming at dawn, alive or not alive." Violence and danger thus crowd out original thought.

Even dramatic entertainment contains a small element of actual physicality that helps replace emotional and intellectual content. Beatty reveals this when he says, "If the drama is bad, if the film says nothing, if the play is hollow, sting me with the theremin, loudly. I'll think I'm responding to the play when it's only a tactile response to vibration. But I don't care. I just like solid entertainment." Like Beatty's hypothetical play, Millie's insipid television serials use irresistibly climactic "thunderstorm[s] of sound" that alone give the impression of plot resolution "even though the people in the walls of the room [have] barely moved."

Vicarious physicality provides a seductive alternative to thought just as the more dangerous actual physicality does. Vicarious physicality also comes in many forms in the novel, from entertainment of what Professor Faber calls "passionate lips and the fist in the stomach" to "the three-dimensional sex magazines," from the graphic violence of the animated White Clown cartoons to the televising of fatal jet car demolition derbies. Common people also go to such races. "Nights when things [get] dull, which [is] every night," the firemen "let loose rats . . . and sometimes chickens, and sometimes cats that would have to be drowned anyway" and bet on which will be the first killed by their eight-legged Mechanical Hound. Occasionally the public voyeurs of violence are treated to television coverage of "dangerous" criminals being similarly hunted down.

Even while Bradbury in the coda warns of intolerant minority pressure, he apparently cannot help but also attack the first type of mass exploitation, that of the simplification of challenges. Most of the coda discusses the way pressure groups threaten free thought by "ripping a page or a paragraph from this book, then that," but some also concerns the simplification of challenging entertainment by exploiting editors. The motive for editors' censoring is sometimes ideological, but it is also sometimes simply economic:

> How do you cram 400 short stories by Twain, Irving, Poe, Maupassant and Bierce into one book?
> Simplicity itself. Skin, debone, demarrow, scarify, melt, render down and destroy. Every adjective that counted, every verb that moved, every metaphor that weighed more than a mosquito—out! Every simile that would have made a submoron's mouth twitch—gone! Any aside that explained the two-bit philosophy of a first-rate writer—lost!
> Every story, slenderized, starved, bluepenciled, leeched and bled white, resemble[s] every other story. Twain read[s] like Poe

read[s] like Shakespeare read[s] like Dostoevsky read[s] like—in
the finale—Edgar Guest. Every word of more than three sylla-
bles [has] been razored. Every image that demand[s] so much as
one instant's attention—shot dead.

The economic rather than ideological motive shown in this impassioned
passage is important to recognize. Although the rest of the coda attacks the
intolerance of minority pressure groups, including editors who have
censored the "controversial" ideas of Bradbury himself, in this instance the
motive of the editors is simply to remove anything requiring even "one
instant's attention." This exploits readers' desires for easy gratification just as
do the "digests-digests, digests-digests-digests," which Beatty in the novel
cites as one of the first examples of simplified challenges.

Certainly present-day American society abounds with examples of the
exploitation Bradbury discusses: the simplification of challenges, both artistic
and educational; an overemphasis of competitive diversions like sports and
contests; rampant drug use; and commodified physicality, both actual and
vicarious. All of these pleasurable pursuits interest us so much that they
threaten to replace independent thought. If it were not for the controversies
over censorship and political correctness, the numerous examples of mass
exploitation in American society might make readers wonder why Bradbury
attacks the real but lesser problem of intolerant pressure groups so much
more vehemently.

Professor Faber says that "books are to remind us what asses and fools
we are." Ray Bradbury's *Fahrenheit 451* certainly fulfills this goal, for it shows
readers more than forty years after its first publication how individual
thought can so easily be supplanted by thoughtless conformity. Bradbury's
warning about the dangers of intolerant minority pressure is perceptive and
important, but it should not overshadow his subtler but more important
warning about mass exploitation. Despite the ease of recognizing the problems of minority pressure in the book, mass exploitation begins earlier,
requires the participation of a far greater majority of the population, and has
a more direct effect on the decline of thought. This should remind us that
even more dangerous than the pressure groups that attempt to peck away at
the freedom of expression and, eventually, thought is our own desire for easy
gratification. The "publishers, exploiters, broadcasters" have great economic
incentive to exploit this desire, and when we allow such pleasurably escapist
mass exploitation to replace our thoughtful interest in the real world, we
abnegate our intellectual and moral responsibilities as human beings.

RAFEEQ O. McGIVERON

"Do You Know the Legend of Hercules and Antaeus?": The Wilderness in Ray Bradbury's Fahrenheit 451

The importance of the wilderness in Ray Bradbury's 1953 ⟨novel⟩ *Fahrenheit 451* has been relatively ignored by critics, and when it has been discussed, this crucial subtheme has been distorted by oversimplification. Many have commented rather briefly upon Bradbury's depiction of the wilderness, but few go beyond seeing, as John Huntington does, that "nature is good and technology is bad." Certainly Bradbury shows nature to be preferable to the artificial sterility of the novel's compulsively hedonistic urban consumer society, yet he also wisely suggests that to be truly human we must know our place in the natural world not only by appreciating the beauties of the wilderness but by respecting its awesome power as well. The thoughtful and moral characters of the novel draw strength from the wilderness, and, when appropriate, they also respect and even fear it. It is this common approach to the world that makes them humane and admirable.

Clarisse McClellan, the inquisitive seventeen year old who helps the dissatisfied "fireman" Guy Montag turn away from his profession of burning books, illustrates how an appreciation of the wilderness helps lead to an understanding of one's place in the natural world. When she is first introduced, Bradbury characterizes her with very positive, lyrical nature imagery. Walking down a moonlit autumnal sidewalk, Clarisse, with her "slender and milk-white" face, seems as if she is "letting the motion of the wind and the

From *Extrapolation* 38, no. 2. © 1997 by Kent State University Press.

leaves carry her forward." Less than two pages later her face is "bright as snow in the moonlight," "fragile milk crystal with a soft and constant light in it." Her eyes are like "two shining drops of bright water," "two miraculous bits of violet amber," and Montag can catch "the faintest breath of fresh apricots and strawberries in the air" even though it is "quite impossible, so late in the year." In the words of Donald Watt, "The meeting with Clarisse . . . introduces a contrast in Bradbury's narrative between the grimy, harsh, destructive milieu of the firemen and the clean, regenerative world of nature." Whereas Montag's colleagues all have "the colors of cinders and ash about them, and the continual smell of burning from their pipes," Clarisse is refreshing in her naturalness.

Just as she is associated so carefully with nature imagery, Clarisse happily and wisely appreciates the natural world. According to Clarisse, most of the scurrying inhabitants of the city fail to notice the natural beauties around them: "I sometimes think drivers don't know what grass is, or flowers, because they never see them slowly. . . . If you showed a driver a green blur, Oh yes! he'd say, that's grass!" Unlike the average citizen, however, Clarisse has seen the sunrise and has noticed the morning dew and the man in the moon. She knows that "rain feels good" and "even tastes good," "just like wine"—a positive thing to Bradbury—and she has found that old leaves "smell like cinnamon." She rubs a dandelion under her chin to discover whether she is in love, and she often "hike[s] around in the forests and watch[es] the birds and collect[s] butterflies." She may kill a few colorful butterflies now and then, but Bradbury merely winks at this old-fashioned form of "appreciation."

Because she makes the effort to appreciate the many beauties of the natural world, Clarisse also has developed a far better understanding of her place in nature than the average person has. Her schoolmates, for example, obviously do not understand their natural capacity for humaneness, for they all are "either shouting or dancing around like wild or beating up one another." In a sense Clarisse truly is "letting the motion of the wind and the leaves carry her forward," for she allows her human nature to guide her. It is natural, for example, for humans to be curious and thoughtful, and one of the first things Montag notices about Clarisse is that her "milk-white" face possesses "a kind of gentle hunger that touch[es] over everything with tireless curiosity." Indeed, she questions much of the compulsive hedonism of her society, not "want[ing] to know *how* a thing was done, but *why*." Considered antisocial, Clarisse must see a psychiatrist regularly, yet she tells Montag, "It's so strange. I'm very social indeed. It all depends on what you mean by social, doesn't it? Social to me means talking to you about things like this." Clarisse's evaluation is correct, of course, her understanding of human nature stemming at least in part from her appreciation of the wilderness.

Clarisse's understanding of her place in nature benefits Montag as well. Occasionally Montag finds "a bouquet of late flowers on his porch, or a handful of chestnuts in a little sack, or some autumn leaves neatly pinned to a sheet of white paper and thumbtacked to his door," all gifts from Clarisse. In addition, more important than mere tokens of friendship, Clarisse's example helps stimulate Montag to wonder and to try new experiences. Even Clarisse notices it, for she tells him that he is unlike the other "firemen" she has met: "When I said something about the moon, you looked at the moon, last night. The others would never do that." Later, made curious by Clarisse, Montag tastes the rain, and at Clarisse's urging he smells the leaves. Though he claims feebly, "It's just I haven't had the time—," Clarisse's example shows him that there is more to life than the moral and intellectual sterility of the unaesthetic workaday world. In other words, she helps him find his own place in the natural world and thereby recognize the potentials of his own human nature.

Fire Captain Beatty, the novel's chief book burner, mockingly derides "that little idiot's routine. . . . Flowers, butterflies, leaves, sunsets, oh, hell! . . . . A few blades of grass and the quarters of the moon. What trash. What good did she ever *do* with all that?" One answer to Beatty's nervous question, of course, is that unlike the majority of the population—Guy's overdosing wife Millie, for example, who sees the wilderness only as a place to "get [the car] up around ninety-five and . . . feel wonderful" hitting rabbits and dogs—Clarisse is truly happy. Whereas Beatty and the "firemen" burn down homes found to contain books while the owners are taken "screaming off to the insane asylum," Clarisse and her example help Montag learn to think again. Even Bradbury in his Afterword admits that Clarisse "verg[es] on silly starstruck chatter," but there can be little doubt that her simple appreciation of the wilderness nevertheless strengthens her humanity and Montag's also.

Donald Watt has noted that Faber, the old former literature professor who helps Montag learn to think again, is associated with "nature and natural smells." Although Faber "look[s] as if he ha[s] not been out of the house in years," Montag, significantly, first met Faber in a "green park a year ago." "They had sat in the soft green light. . . . His name was Faber, and when he finally lost his fear of Montag, he talked in a cadenced voice, looking at the sky and the trees and the green park." Along with symbolically associating Faber with nature, Bradbury demonstrates that the professor, like Clarisse—and unlike the mindless majority—appreciates the natural world and understands his place in it.

Even Faber's relationship to books is depicted with appreciative nature imagery. When Montag brings a Bible to Faber's house, Faber smells it lovingly: "Do you know that books smell like nutmeg or some spice from a foreign land? I loved to smell them when I was a boy." Watt, of course, already has drawn attention to this imagery of "natural smells." In addition, however, Faber describes books with a nice piece of visual nature imagery as well. According to Faber, "This book can go under the microscope. You'd find life under the glass, streaming past in infinite profusion." Though he is speaking figuratively, the vehicle of the metaphor is as valid as the tenor. A book is the product of technological manufacturing processes just as, say, the novel's four-walled televisors are, yet it is a coarser, homier kind of artifact, rough wood pulp rather than fired glass and vacuum-sealed electronics. Whereas Beatty praises fire for being "clean" and "antibiotic," Faber recognizes that humans are a part of nature and thus directly opposes such unnatural sterility, even at the microscopic and metaphorical level. Faber's microscope metaphor is surely the most subtle and unexpected piece of imagery tying together books and an understanding of the natural world, and to my taste it is also the most thematically effective.

In associating books with the natural world, Faber reflects Bradbury's narrative, wherein they are described with more poetic nature imagery. Throughout the novel books are "pigeon-winged," like "white pigeon[s] . . . [with] wings fluttering," "like slaughtered birds" whose pages are like "snowy feather[s]," and "like roasted birds, their wings ablaze with red and yellow feathers." Furthermore, Bradbury links books with nature again when Montag in a feverish daze takes the subway to Faber's house, illegal Bible in plain view in his hands, and the disillusioned "fireman" attempts in vain to consider the lilies of the field of Matthew 6:28.

In addition to employing this type of nature imagery, Bradbury eventually has Faber make the connection between humanity and the wilderness explicit. The old man asks Montag, "Do you know the legend of Hercules and Antaeus, the giant wrestler, whose strength was incredible so long as he stood firmly on the earth? But when he was held, rootless, in midair, by Hercules, he perished easily. If there isn't something in that legend for us today, in this city, in our time, then I am completely insane." Clearly Faber is not insane. He sees that "flowers are trying to live on flowers, instead of growing on good rain and black loam," because people refuse to recognize that "even fireworks, for all their prettiness, come from the chemistry of the earth." Faber knows that humanity cannot "grow, feeding on flowers and fireworks, without completing the cycle back to reality." Unlike Millie and Beatty, Faber appreciates the wilderness, and he knows his place in it as well.

After Montag finally kills the taunting, suicidal Beatty, he escapes into the wilderness which—rather improbably, considering that "there are billions of us and that's too many"—exists just on the edge of the city. Bradbury echoes the important dichotomy that Faber draws between "[t]he comfortable people" and the Antaeuses who understand their place in the natural world. Montag imagines the people of the city with "pale, night-frightened faces, like gray animals peering from electric caves," and when "in a sudden peacefulness" he floats away in the river, he feels "as if he ha[s] left a stage behind and many actors." Bradbury writes, "The river was mild and leisurely, going away from the people who ate shadows for breakfast and steam for lunch and vapors for supper. The river was very real; it held him comfortably and gave him the time at last, the leisure, to consider this month, this year, a lifetime of years." Whereas the city is shrouded by "the seven veils of unreality" and "the walls of [television] parlors," here "cows [chew] grass and pigs [sit] in warm ponds at noon and dogs [bark] after white sheep on a hill." In the words of William F. Touponce, Montag journeys to "the real natural world . . . outside the narcissism of the city," a place where people can have "a non-alienating relationship to nature."

Montag's flight from the city—which, coincidentally, is about to be atom-bombed by one of the many faceless enemies of an America that has "started and won two atomic wars since 1990"—reveals unmistakable imagery of the appreciation of the wilderness. When Montag startles a deer, Bradbury unleashes a heavy half-page of lingering description:

> He smelled the heavy musk like perfume mingled with the gummed exhalation of the animal's breath, all cardomom and moss and ragweed odor . . .
>
> There must have been a billion leaves on the land; he waded in them, a dry river smelling of hot cloves and warm dust. And the other smells! There was a smell like a cut potato from all the land, raw and cold and white from having the moon on it most of the night. There was a smell like pickles from a bottle and a smell of parsley on the table at home. There was a faint yellow odor like mustard from a jar. There was a smell like carnations from the yard next door. He put down his hand and felt a weed rise up like a child brushing him. His fingers smelled of licorice.
>
> He stood breathing, and the more he breathed the land in, the more he was filled up with all the details of the land. He was not empty. There was more than enough here to fill him. There would always be more than enough.

John Huntington suggests that Bradbury's "purple rhetoric obscures true perception," and there is some truth in this. Some particulars may indeed be

overdone, examples of what Kingsley Amis calls "dime-a-dozen sensitivity";
certainly the idea of an endearing, child-like *weed* that smells like licorice is
syrupy sweet. Yet despite such occasional problems of heavy-handed execution, Bradbury's emphasis on the necessity of appreciating the wilderness
should not be dismissed so easily.

As with Clarisse and Faber, this appreciation helps lead Montag to an
understanding of his place in the natural world. Soon Montag "know[s]
himself as a [sic] animal come from the forest. . . . He [is] a thing of brush
and liquid eye, of fur and muzzle and hoof, he [is] a thing of horn and blood
that would smell like autumn if you bled it out on the ground." Though
Huntington must "take it that somehow this reduction of the human to
animal is somehow consoling and ennobling," it really requires no special
stretch of the imagination to see it as such. Clarisse already has demonstrated
that to truly appreciate the wilderness is to have a better understanding of
one's own humanity, and Faber has asserted that one must not forget that
humans are a product of and a part of the natural world. Rather than
"reduce" the human, Bradbury with this new image merely has linked it
more explicitly with nature.

While Montag is still in the city, Bradbury's nature imagery consists
mainly of that given by Clarisse and Faber. Once Montag escapes and begins
to experience the wilderness for himself, however, Bradbury uses not only
"purple rhetoric" but imagery appropriate to respect and awe as well. In
Bradbury's scheme, the wilderness is not simply "good" and "nurturing"
(Huntington), a "refuge" (David Mogen), "a regenerative world" (Watt), "an
arcadian utopia" (Touponce), or "a new Eden" (Willis E. McNelly); indeed,
it can be all of those, but the wilderness is also a force to be humbly
respected. The only critic to have commented upon this previously is George
Edgar Slusser, who merely notes with tantalizing brevity that nature is dark,
overwhelming, and immense. Examining Bradbury's awed treatment of the
wilderness in some detail is worthwhile, however, for it reveals a significant
attitude of humility and respect.

Bradbury shows that the second aspect of truly understanding one's
place in nature is being humbled by the vastness and power of the wilderness.
When Montag first sees the stars in the wilderness, undimmed by the light
pollution of the city, he sees not the pretty twinkling lights that readers
might expect but "a great juggernaut of stars form in the sky and threaten to
crush him." Though the river in which he floats seems comforting, the land
seems a threatening creature: "He looked in at the great black creature
without eyes or light, without shape, with only a size that went a thousand
miles, without wanting to stop, with its grass hills and forests that were
waiting for him." It is difficult to read this description as majestic or inviting,

for the land's nightmarish darkness, its vast size, and its "waiting" seem brooding and ominous instead. When Montag finally steps ashore, the enormity of the wilderness is humbling: "The land rushed at him, a tidal wave. He was crushed by darkness and the look of the country and the million odors on a wind that iced the body. He fell back under the breaking wave of darkness and sound and smell, his ears roaring." Bradbury compares the "dark land rising" to "the largest wave in the history of remembering," which in his youth "slammed him down in salt mud and green darkness, water burning mouth and nose, retching his stomach, screaming! Too much water!" The ocean was fearsome to the child, and now to the adult there seems "too much land." Even the passage with the majestic, startled deer and the licorice-smelling weed that "rise[s] up like a child" describes the wilderness as a "huge night where trees ran at him, pulled away, ran, pulled away to the pulse of the heart behind his eyes"—definitely no "flowers, butterflies, leaves, sunsets" here.

Stumbling upon disused railroad tracks, Montag meets a former professor "significantly named Granger, a farmer, a shepherd guiding his flock [of book-memorizing intellectuals]" (McNelly). In a rather lengthy aside, Granger tells Montag about his grandfather, who

> hoped that someday our cities would open up more and let the green and the land and the wilderness in more, to remind people that we're allotted a little space on earth and that we survive in that wilderness that can take back what it has given, as easily as blowing its breath on us or sending the sea to tell us we are not so big. When we forget how close the wilderness is in the night . . . someday it will come in and get us, for we will have forgotten how terrible and real it can be.

While this passage seems to begin with mere appreciation, it soon shifts to humility and respect even more marked than that of Faber's story of Hercules. Though Granger's assertion that an "atom-bomb mushroom" seen from a V-2 rocket two hundred miles up is "a pin-prick . . . nothing . . . with wilderness all around it" now seems dated in the age of the hydrogen bomb, in a wider sense his attitude of humility and respect toward a wilderness that might "someday . . . come in and get us" is still justified. Almost half a century after Bradbury wrote, the ravages of nature's "breath" may be more predictable, but they are no more controllable; moreover, if the camera in the nose of the V-2 were rotated up to look into the "juggernaut of stars," with its climate-wrecking meteors, its supernovas, and its quasars, Granger's awe of nature's power would seem even more justified.

Despite such evidence of respect and even fear, Bradbury's last use of natural imagery is a comforting one. As Montag and the other book-memorizers walk back toward the atom-bombed city, blithely unconcerned with radiation poisoning, he remembers a passage from Revelations: *"And on the other side of the river was there a tree of life, which bore twelve manner of fruits, and yielded her fruit every month: and the leaves of the tree were for the healing of the nations."* This final piece of imagery reminds us, perhaps more directly than any other, that even though the natural world may be vast and sometimes threatening, it still can be a source of strength.

Bradbury's treatment of the wilderness in *Fahrenheit 451* is more complex and more true to life than it might first appear. Though his loving description of the wilderness and his persistent use of positive nature imagery clearly suggest that we should appreciate the natural beauties around us, Bradbury's careful reminders that the wilderness is vast and powerful should not be ignored. To be truly human we must know our place in the natural world, not only appreciating the wilderness but humbly respecting it, too. The humanity of Clarisse and Faber and Granger and Montag illustrate the benefits of understanding this—and the suicidal tendencies of the anesthetized Millie and the bitterly jesting Beatty reveal the grave dangers of forgetting it.

Chronology

1920   Ray Bradbury born August 22 in Waukegan, Illinois. He is the third son of Leonard Spaulding Bradbury, an electrical lineman, and Esther Marie Moberg Bradbury, a native-born Swede. His twin brothers, Leonard and Samuel, had been born in 1916; Samuel died in 1918.

1926   A sister, Elizabeth, is born; the family moves to Tucson, Arizona, in the fall.

1927   Elizabeth dies of pneumonia and the family returns to Waukegan in May.

1928   Discovers science fiction in *Amazing Stories.*

1931   Writes first stories on butcher paper.

1932   Leonard Bradbury is laid off from his job as a telephone lineman, and the family moves back to Tucson; Ray performs as an amateur magician at Oddfellows Hall and American Legion; reads comics to children on radio station KGAR.

1933   Family returns to Waukegan; Ray sees Century of Progress exhibit at Chicago World's Fair.

1934	Seeking employment, father moves family to Los Angeles where Ray works as "live audience" for the Burns and Allen radio show.
1937	Acts as scriptwriter, producer, and director of the *Roman Review* at Los Angeles High School; joins the Los Angeles Science Fiction League.
1938	Graduates from high school; first short story, "Hollerbochen's Dilemma," published in *Imagination!*
1939	Publishes his own fan magazine, *Futuria Fantasia*; attends World Science Fiction Convention in New York; joins actress Laraine Day's drama group, the Wilshire Players Guild; sells newspapers on Los Angeles street corner, a job he keeps until 1942.
1940	"It's Not the Heat It's the Hu . . ." published in *Rob Wagner's Script Magazine* on November 2.
1941	Participates in Robert Heinlein's weekly writing class; "Pendulum," co-authored with Henry Hasse, published in *Super Science Stories*.
1942	Begins earning $20 a week writing short stories and decides to quit selling newpapers to write full-time; his story "The Lake" is the first to exhibit his distinctive style.
1945	Begins publishing in "slick" magazines; travels to Mexico; "The Big Black and White Game" included in *Best American Short Stories*.
1947	Marries Marguerite McClure; publishes first book, *Dark Carnival*; "Homecoming" wins O. Henry Award and is published in *Prize Stories of 1947*; becomes client of literary agent Don Congdon.
1948	"Powerhouse" wins O. Henry Award; "I See You Never" selected for *Best American Short Stories 1948*.
1949	Selected as "best author of 1949" for fantasy and science fiction by the National Fantasy Fan Federation; first daughter born.

1950   *The Martian Chronicles* published; republished in London as *The Silver Locusts*, 1951.

1951   *The Illustrated Man* published; republished London, 1952; second daughter born.

1952   Writes *It Came from Outer Space*; "The Other Foot" published in *Best American Short Stories*.

1953   *The Golden Apples of the Sun* and *Fahrenheit 451* published; travels to Ireland, stays six months to write screenplay for John Huston's *Moby Dick*; wins Benjamin Franklin Award for year's best short story published in a popular magazine.

1954   Awarded $1,000 from American Academy of Arts and Letters for contributions to American literature.

1955   *Switch on the Night*, a children's book, published; *The October Country* published; third daughter born.

1956   *Dandelion Wine* and *Sun and Shadow* published. Leonard Bradbury dies.

1958   Fourth daughter born.

1959   *A Medicine for Melancholy* published; "The Day It Rained Forever" is selected for *Best American Short Stories*.

1962   *Something Wicked This Way Comes, The Small Assassin*, and *R Is for Rocket* published.

1963   Receives Academy Award nomination for *Icarus Montgolfier Wright*; publishes first collection of drama, *The Anthem Sprinters and Other Antics*.

1964   *The Machineries of Joy: Short Stories* and *The Pedestrian* published; *American Journey*, his film history of the nation, opens at the New York World's Fair; produces *The World of Ray Bradbury* at the Coronet Theatre, Los Angeles.

1965   Produces *The Wonderful Ice Cream Suit* in Los Angeles; *The World of Ray Bradbury* has brief, unsuccessful run in New York. "The Other Foot" selected for *Fifty Best American Short Stories: 1915–1965*. *The Autumn People* published by Ballantine; *The Vintage Bradbury* published by Random House.

1966   Francois Truffaut's movie *Fahrenheit 451* released; *Twice Twenty-Two, Tomorrow Midnight* and *S Is for Space* published; Esther Moberg Bradbury dies.

1967   *Dandelion Wine* produced as musical drama at Lincoln Center; *The Anthem Sprinters*, a collection of Irish plays, produced at Beverly Hills Playhouse.

1968   Wins Aviation-Space Writers Association award for "An Impatient Gulliver above Our Roots," a science article published in *Life Magazine*.

1969   Film version of *The Illustrated Man* released; *I Sing the Body Electric! Stories* published; *Christus Apollo*, a cantata, performed at UCLA.

1970   "Mars Is Heaven!" selected for the Science Fiction Hall of Fame by the Science Fiction Writers of America.

1972   *The Wonderful Ice Cream Suit and Other Plays* and *The Halloween Tree* published; *Madrigals for the Space Age*, for Mixed Chorus and Narrator with Piano Accompaniment, published.

1973   *When Elephants Last in the Dooryard Bloomed*, Bradbury's first collection of poetry, published.

1975   *Pillar of Fire and Other Plays* published.

1976   *Long After Midnight* published.

1977   *Where Robot Mice and Robot Men Run Round in Robot Towns*, a collection of poetry, published; receives Life Achievement Award at the World Fantasy Convention.

1980   *The Stories of Ray Bradbury* and "The Last Circus and The Electrocution" published; receives Gandolf Award as "Grand Master" at the Hugo Award Ceremonies.

1981   *The Haunted Computer and the Android Pope*, a collection of poetry, published.

1982   *The Complete Poems of Ray Bradbury* and *The Love Affair* published.

1983   *Dinosaur Tales* published.

1984   Film version of *Something Wicked This Way Comes*, screenplay by Bradbury, released; *Forever and the Earth: Radio Dramatization* published. A collection of early mystery stories, *A Memory of Murder*, published; receives Jules Verne Award; receives Valentine Davies Award from the Writers Guild of America for his work in films.

1985   *Death Is a Lonely Business* published.

1987   *Death Has Lost Its Charm For Me*, poems, published.

1988   *The Toynbee Convector*, a collection of stories, published.

1989   *The Climate of Palettes* published.

1990   Published *The Day It Rained Forever* (a musical), *A Graveyard for Lunatics* (a novel), *Another Tale of Two Cities* (novel), *Zen and the Art of Writing* (a collection of essays on the art and craft of writing).

1991   *Yestermorrow: Obvious Answers to Impossible Futures*, essays, published.

1992   *Green Shadows, White Whale*, a novel, published.

1993   "The Stars," a poem, published.

1996   *Quicker Than the Eye*, a collection of stories, published.

1997   *Driving Blind*, a collection of stories; two poems, "Dogs Think that Every Day is Christmas" and "With Cat for Comforter" published.

Contributors

HAROLD BLOOM is Sterling Professor of the Humanities at Yale University and Henry W. and Albert A. Berg Professor of English at the New York University Graduate School. He is the author of over 20 books, including *Shelley's Mythmaking* (1959), *The Visionary Company* (1961), *Blake's Apocalypse* (1963), *Yeats* (1970), *A Map of Misreading* (1975), *Kabbalah and Criticism* (1975), *Agon: Toward a Theory of Revisionism* (1982), *The American Religion* (1992), *The Western Canon* (1994), and *Omens of Millennium: The Gnosis of Angels, Dreams, and Resurrection* (1996). *The Anxiety of Influence* (1973) sets forth Professor Bloom's provocative theory of the literary relationships between the great writers and their predecessors. His most recent books include *Shakespeare: The Invention of the Human*, a 1998 National Book Award finalist, and *How to Read and Why*, which was published in 2000. In 1999, Professor Bloom received the prestigious American Academy of Arts and Letters Gold Medal for Criticism.

WAYNE L. JOHNSON is the author of *Ray Bradbury* (1980). He has contributed articles and essays to numerous journals, and contributed to the collection *Critical Encounters: Writers and Themes in Science Fiction* (1978).

DONALD WATT is professor of English at the State University College of New York at Geneseo. He has edited *The Collected Poetry of Aldous Huxley: The Critical Heritage* (1971), and has written articles for several journals. He is a contributor to *Isaac Asimov* in the WRITERS OF THE 21ST CENTURY series.

WILLIAM F. TOUPONCE has written several critical articles on the works of Ray Bradbury and has recently written for the journal *Children's Literature*.

SUSAN SPENCER is an instructor in the Department of English at the University of Central Oklahoma.

DAVID SEED is a lecturer in the Department of English Language and Literature at the University of Liverpool, England.

KEVIN HOSKINSON is associate professor of developmental English at Lorain County Community College in Elyria, Ohio. His teaching and scholarly research focus upon 20th century American literature and Irish drama.

RAFEEQ O. McGIVERON is an instructor of English at Lansing Community College in Lansing, Michigan. His articles on Robert A. Heinlein, Robert Silverberg, Ray Bradbury, and Amy Lowell have been published in *Extrapolation, Science-Fiction Studies, The Explicator,* and *Critique.*

Bibliography

Amis, Kingsley. *New Maps of Hell: A Survey of Science Fiction.* New York: Arno, 1975.

Bloom, Harold, ed. *Ray Bradbury.* Philadelphia: Chelsea House, 2001.

Greenberg, Martin Harry, and Joseph D. Olander, eds. *Ray Bradbury.* New York: Taplinger, 1980.

Hamblin, Charles F. "Bradbury's *Fahrenheit 451* in the Classroom." *English Journal* 57, no. 6 (September 1968): 818–19.

Hienger, Jorg. "The Uncanny and Science Fiction," translated by Elsa Schneider. *Science Fiction Studies* 6, no. 18 (1979): 144–52.

Huntington, John. "Utopian and Anti-Utopian Logic: H. G. Wells and His Successors." *Science-Fiction Studies* 9 (1982): 122–46.

Jacobs, Robert. "Interview with Ray Bradbury," *The Writer's Digest* 55, no. 2 (February 1976): 18–25.

Johnson, Wayne L. *Ray Bradbury.* New York: Frederick Ungar, 1980.

Mogen, David. *Ray Bradbury.* Boston: Twayne, 1986.

Moskowitz, Sam. *Seekers of Tomorrow, Masters of Modern Science Fiction.* New York: Ballantine, 1967.

Nolan, William F. *The Bradbury Companion: A Life and Career History, Photolog, and Comprehensive Checklist of Writings with Facsimiles from Ray Bradbury's Unpublished and Uncollected Work in All Media.* Detroit: Gale Research, 1975.

Riley, Robert. "The Artistry of Ray Bradbury." *Extrapolation* 13 (1971): 64–74.

Sisario, Peter. "A Study of the Allusions in Bradbury's *Fahrenheit 451.*" *English Journal* 59, no. 2 (February 1970): 201–05.

Slusser, George Edgar. *The Bradbury Chronicles.* San Bernardino, Calif.: Borgo Press, 1977.

Touponce, William F. *Ray Bradbury and the Poetics of Reverie: Fantasy, Science Fiction, and the Reader.* Ann Arbor, Mich.: UMI Research Press, 1984.

Warrick, Patricia S. and Martin Harry Greenberg, eds. *The New Awareness: Religion Through Science Fiction.* New York: Delacorte Press, 1975.

Acknowledgments

"Machines of Joy and Sorrow: Rockets, Time Machines, Robots, Man vs. Machine, Orwellian Tales, and *Fahrenheit 451*" by Wayne L. Johnson. From *Ray Bradbury*. © 1980 by Frederick Ungar Publishing Co., Inc. Reprinted with permission.

"Burning Bright: *Fahrenheit 451* as Symbolic Dystopia" by Donald Watt. From *Ray Bradbury*, Martin Harry Greenberg and Joseph D. Olander, eds. © 1980 by Martin Harry Greenberg and Joseph D. Olander. Reprinted with permission.

"Reverie and the Marvelous: Doublings of the Self in *The Martian Chronicles* and *Fahrenheit 451*" by William F. Touponce from *Ray Bradbury and the Poetics of Reverie: Fantasy, Science Fiction, and the Reader*. © 1984, 1981 by William Ferdinand Touponce. Reprinted with permission.

"The Post-Apocalyptic Library: Oral and Literate Culture in *Fahrenheit 451* and *A Canticle for Leibowitz*" by Susan Spencer. From *Extrapolation* 32, no. 4. (Winter 1991): 331–42. © 1991 by The Kent State University Press. Reprinted with permission.

"The Flight from the Good Life: *Fahrenheit 451* in the Context of Postwar American Dystopias" by David Seed. From *Journal of American Studies* 28, no. 2 (August 1994): 225–40. © 1994 by the Cambridge University Press. Reprinted with permission.

140 ACKNOWLEDGMENTS

"*The Martian Chronicles* and *Fahrenheit 451:* Ray Bradbury's Cold War Novels" by Kevin Hoskinson. From *Extrapolation* 36, no. 4. (Winter 1995): 347–57. © 1995 by The Kent State University Press. Reprinted with permission.

"The Imagery of Hands in *Fahrenheit 451*" by Rafeeq O. McGiveron. From *The Explicator* 54, no. 3 (Spring 1996): 177–80. (Original title: "Bradbury's *Fahrenheit 451.*") © 1996 by Heldref Publications. Reprinted with permission.

"What 'Carried the Trick'? Mass Exploitation and the Decline of Thought in Ray Bradbury's *Fahrenheit 451*" by Rafeeq O. McGiveron. From *Extrapolation* 37, no. 3 (Fall 1996): 245–256. © 1996 by The Kent State University Press. Reprinted with permission.

"'Do You Know the Legend of Hercules and Antaeus?' The Wilderness in Ray Bradbury's *Fahrenheit 451*" by Rafeeq O. McGiveron. From *Extrapolation* 38, no. 2 (Summer 1997): 102–109. © 1997 by The Kent State University Press. Reprinted with permission.

Index

ATE DUE

GAYLORD			PRINTED IN U.S.A.

JAN   '08